Harvest of the Heart

*As long as the earth endures,
seedtime and harvest will never cease.*

—Genesis 8:22

Lena Milton

A man belongs to the plans of his heart

—Proverbs 16:1

Copyright © 2010 by Lena Milton.

Library of Congress Control Number: 2010913478
ISBN: Hardcover   978-1-4535-7462-1
              Softcover   978-1-4535-7461-4

All rights reserved. No part of this book may be reproduced or transmitted in any form or by any means, electronic or mechanical, including photocopying, recording, or by any information storage and retrieval system, without permission in writing from the copyright owner.

This book was printed in the United States of America.

To order additional copies of this book, contact:
Xlibris Corporation
1-888-795-4274
www.Xlibris.com
Orders@Xlibris.com
59776

CONTENTS

Author's Note 7
Acknowledgements 10
Introduction: Harvest of the Heart 12

Chapter 1: The Kingdom of God 27
Chapter 2: Light on the Material World 34
Chapter 3: Creative Power 38
Chapter 4: Light on Love and Fear 46
Chapter 5: Light on the Blessed Life 52
Chapter 6: Light on Faith 73
    The Root of Faith 73
    According to His Will 80
    Borrowed Faith v. Grounded Faith 83
    Grounded Faith 89
    Borrowed Faith 90
Chapter 7: The Law of Return 94
Chapter 8: The Tree of Life 101

Chapter 9: Health: The Law of Life 109
    Mind over Matter.. 131
    Your Body, behind Enemy Lines 139
    Metamorphosis: Out with the Old, in with the New 143
    Restoration... 156

Chapter 10: An illustration from Job............................ 159
Chapter 11: The Power of Words 172
Chapter 12: The Heart of Life 189
Chapter 13: God's Will Be Done.................................. 193
Chapter 14: The Spirit's Call.. 207
Chapter 15: The Power of Forgiveness 220
Chapter 16: The Power Within..................................... 237
Chapter 17: Breaking the Cycle 245
Chapter 18: Unity 256

Author's Note... 269

Author's Note

For wisdom will enter your heart, and knowledge will be pleasant to your soul. Discretion will protect you and understanding will guard you.
—Proverbs 2:10-11

Let me just begin by saying that I could never begin to understand how God's vision and the desire to carry it out was placed so gently in the secret places of my heart. Never would I have pursued this path in my own strength because before this wisdom came to me, I had no knowledge in regards to spiritual principles and laws that govern all living things that he has revealed to me through his word.

Before this revelation, I prayed through emergencies only. I became an eyesore to many people as I deliberately destroyed their peace of mind through manipulation and deceit. My education was limited and I did more than my share of drugs. In fact, the last thing that I said to God was; 'God, I'll be right back' in my pursuit of an alternative life style to say the least, so yes, I often wondered why he chose me. Who would believe me?

Within these past few years, God's word have nurtured and developed the task that was set before me while there has been more than a few occasions where I have felt that it was too big for me to handle and gave up. I remember thinking at one point that this just might be a set up creatively orchestrated by Satan himself in attempts to destroy me altogether along with all of my readers. God describes him as a thief that has been known to take the good things that God has created for our benefit and put his twist on it, so that it has the appearance of truth with no truth behind it.

But then I would think about the thousands of hours I have spent meditating on the things that he revealed to me. How my life and everything around me corresponded with this truth, which reaffirmed what I've learned. No, this had to be God, because the devil wouldn't reveal to me the very things that would improve my level of comfort in this world and destroy his work altogether.

Through my intense study of the bible, my life and all its intricacies have been explained to me and within this truth was my deliverance. I began to see why God would choose someone like me, so that through me, he would reveal his power of complete restoration and redemption. The fact that I was a cracked pot qualified me as fit for use. That the greatness of his work might be revealed for the world to see and come to understand that God loves us In spite of who we are, not because of who we are. If I was qualified by man's standard, you might deem my information credible based on what I have learned through education and experience. No, this was all the work of God because the wisdom that I have been entrusted with far exceeds classroom education.

My information may intrigue you, or it may at a glance become a bit incredulous because it will most certainly oppose everything you have ever known as truth. But if your life and way of thinking corresponds to the nature of this book and you have an intense desire to learn more, then God has chosen you to receive this message of hope.

Acknowledgements

How could I thank anyone before giving thanks to God in heaven for saving me from a life of destruction, for giving me hope through his word and using me as vessel to which his word has been entrusted.

A special thanks to my mother Delita Milton for being a living example of strength, hope, and perseverance. Throughout my life you have taught me through your actions the significance of giving and unconditional love. It is because of your dedication to help not only your family, but to also bring some level of comfort to all the people you service in your day to day life that is responsible for the nurturing of this vision.

I would also like to thank my father James Milton for introducing me to the God I now serve and for all the spiritual encouragement you have given me throughout the years.

I dedicate this book first to my children; Nigel, Selina and Carina. My hope is that you come to a complete understanding of who you are in Christ and the victory you have through him. May you grow to love him and dedicate yourselves to a life of service.

This book is also written in special honor of my sister Desiree and my brother Jamie and all my relatives near and far, who have been oppressed by disease or hopelessness. May the teachings of this book be engraved in your heart as a weapon against defeat. That through it, you may rise up against all adversity and overcome them by declaring the victory you have in Christ by faith. And for those who have already been delivered from the grips of death through faith, may the wisdom within this book contribute to your understanding.

Thanks to Mary Jarvis and Rose Alconga of Xlibris Publishing for being so patient with me, who took the time to talk me through my fears and through persistence, encouraged me to release this dream.

This is my contribution to the world.

Introduction

Harvest of the Heart

As long as the earth endures, seedtime and harvest, cold and heat, summer and winter, day and night will never cease.

—Genesis 8:22

Seedtime and Harvest

When tempted, no one should say, "God is tempting me." For God cannot be tempted by evil, nor does he tempt anyone; <u>but each one is tempted when, by his own evil desire, he is dragged away and enticed. Then, after desire has conceived, it gives birth to sin; and sin, when it is full-grown, gives birth to death.</u>

—Jas 1:13-15

In you lies a visualizing entity where all things are possible and where all things currently exist by simply thinking about it. It has always been and forever will be *mind over matter*. The universe was created on this very concept: God being the mind that created the matter, and we, being made in his likeness, live by this very same principle. This is the foundation on which *seedtime and harvest* was established.

Your surroundings, circumstances, mishaps, and the successes that you have experienced in your personal life have been preserved in your subconscious mind, having accepted them as truth. And just as natural seeds produce in accordance to the nature of seed sown, so does our thoughts. The lives we live, our circumstances reflect all that have been sown on the inside of us.

As seedtime and harvest relates to natural farming, human life and all its affairs are built into the same principles and both are governed by the law of return.

Just as love is responsible for the development and growth of all living things, hate on the other hand, is just as powerful and is reciprocal to love and will destroy anything that has life in it. Life and all its intricacies hang upon both laws and will produce a life in accordance to the nature of the thought that is sown.

This has been a spiritual fact from the beginning and was the ministry of Christ.

The truth is; our future will always be determined from our present state of mind. We can never rise above our mental attitude of what we *believe* we can achieve. Nor can we obtain anything in life without thinking it first. We live according to our thoughts, and so we live out our thoughts therefore, the life we live will always be a corresponding reflection of all that exists on the inside of us. Whatever you *believe* is true for you will, by spiritual law, come to you.

In life's simplest terms, one cannot plant an apple tree in a garden and receive oranges as a result. An apple seed is designed to produce apples, and so it is with life. Bad food promotes poor health; good food promotes good health. Bad words promote hate; good words promote love. By this principle, we plant our health, we plant our death, we plant our disease, and in all these things, our circumstances become our destiny to which our faith in our thoughts and actions have brought us, life's ripened fruit, the harvest in which we most certainly reap. The crop simply depends on the farmer.

But if we can begin to grasp this truth and apply it to everything that has developed into our lives, we will not only come to the disturbing realization that all we have that currently exists in our personal lives as well as our social life is a direct reflection of what we have planted in our heart, but also, we will come to realize that we are makers of our own circumstances, but with in this revelation, you will find the problem and solution to most every situation pertaining to life.

In light of this truth, we can now begin to consciously create a life more desirable by first understanding that every thought, word, and deed is indeed a seed, and when we apply the seedtime and harvest law to life, our minds and motives become manufacturing centers for the seed/thoughts sown.

This law governs every aspect of our lives, and by this truth, our words become the harvest of our thoughts, and in the same way, our life becomes the harvest of our words; they follow suit. Everything in life grows into a higher form of expression, and it's because of this law that there are no limits to how far a person may fall or what they can achieve. This proof is evident in everyday life. If this were not true, then all that we intentionally set out to do will remain in its undeveloped state. No, in everything we accomplish, there is always someone else that will take it to the next level, but it all starts with some kind of seed, whether it be in idea, thought or action.

Just as a plant cannot bring forth its fruit without the seed being planted in the ground first, the same thing is true regarding human life. Every word, act, or deed is a seed created from our thoughts, planted into our hearts, and the fruit thereof is a direct result of what we have retained.

The good man brings good things out of the good stored up in him, and the evil man brings evil things out of the evil stored up in him.

—Matthew 12:35

This truth may be hard for many to accept, given the conclusion that *we* create the conditions of our lives for ourselves, if we are living under condemnation, living in impurity, hatred, jealousy, drunkenness, poverty, disease, or defeat, they are a reflection of all we have accepted, in addition to the choices we make ourselves in either thought or action. Good or bad, consciously or subconsciously, your thoughts belong to you, and so they return to you in physical formation as a manifestation of the thoughts that were retained or sent.

Scripture refers to one's life being consumed in affliction as one being under a curse, not by God, but out of disobedience to his words, commands, and decrees. You can find this truth in Deuteronomy 28:15 among many others throughout the Old and New Testaments.

When one chooses to Live their life without God is equivalent to choosing to live under the curse. The reason I say this Is because when one's mind become oblivious to the nature of God, he misses out on the secret wisdom in regards to the power we have in Christ to escape destruction and part of that wisdom is the spiritual laws that operate in our lives everyday.

Adam was not equipped for spiritual battle at the time of creation because God had not yet revealed the spiritual principles to him. That was for a later day, retained in the tree of knowledge, of good and evil. So his only protection was obedience. But when he decided to disobey God, he fell under the curse of destruction non the less.

How people fail in life has not so much to do with their lack of education in regards to the things of this natural world in as much as it does their lack of understanding in regard to the spiritual principles that govern life, but also their lack of obedience to God's commands and instructions.

We all have a hard time at first accepting that we may be responsible for our own disasters and, even more so, contribute to our children's destruction. But it is because of our own ignorance in regard to life and the spiritual principles that govern it, our children's suffering becomes the by-product of our lack of knowledge in the things we as parents have failed to seek and understand. We cannot give them what we don't have; therefore, as children, they suffer the consequences of our bad choices, and as adults, they suffer defeat in every area of life due to their inherited ignorance.

Thoughts of our children suffering, dying, or being killed, the consequences of not being able to pay our bills; fear of losing our job; thoughts of inheriting a genetic disease, alcoholism, obesity; thoughts of poverty, the corresponding emotions that accompanied those thoughts, created the pictures or patterns needed for our mental observation of the thing feared and it is this inward development process that becomes the catalyst for its reality from physical ailments to material possessions.

Images created in the human mind afforded by the thoughts we allow ourselves to entertain is all the mind needs to lay the foundation for its development, and as life proceeds, it attracts to itself like thoughts and pictures that will agree with the thoughts or opinions that are already stored. This is spiritual farming. Its the foundation being laid in preparation of the seed/thought that was sown into your heart. The product is being developed whether a person is conscious of it or not, It's the spiritual law of seedtime and harvest.

Because of our lack of understanding in regards to our soul and its spiritual components, it is much easier to believe that many of our undesired circumstance or conditions would've happened regardless of our thoughts, that they were destined to come given the circumstances rather than considering the mental material that is responsible for the condition that was brought forth.

It would be logical to assume that problems and circumstances appear when the condition presents itself due to no fault of our own, that it just appears out of thin air or that God caused it because he allowed it. But the truth is in many cases, we thought of it with fear of having to go through it or similar circumstances long before the conditions presented itself. The thought correlated with its object and simply produced after its kind. Keep in mind that everything in thought, word, or deed is a seed sown destined for expression and will by spiritual law produce a harvest of its very nature. A tree is known by its fruit.

> *"Make a tree good and its fruit will be good, or make a tree bad and its fruit will be bad, for a tree is recognized by its fruit. You brood of vipers, how can you who are evil say anything good? For out of the overflow of the heart the mouth speaks. The good man brings good things out of the good stored up in him, and the evil man brings evil things out of the evil stored up in him. But I tell you that men will have to give account on the Day of Judgment for every careless word they have spoken. For by your words you will be acquitted, and by your words you will be condemned."*
>
> —Matthew 12: 33-37

Day of Judgment: I believe Christ is referring to the accountability of our words on the day of affliction. He says we will have to give an account of every careless word and by them we are either acquitted or condemned. Keep in mind that he refers to our words as seeds and our words are and outward expression of our thoughts which is the evil or good we store within us. Therefore, he holds us accountable for every careless word spoken, but not later on judgement day as some may assume, but now through the affliction that came as a direct result. We are held accountable and must accept it. Our future comfort is dependent upon this revelation.

Careless words like; you're killing me, you make me sick, I never have enough, you're just like you're no good father/mother. By these words you are condemned in your troubles. But words such as; I'm healthy, wealthy and strong, God always provide for me, life is good, my kids will grow up in God, things may seem to be going bad, but they're not. By these words you escape the troubles of this world and is therefore acquitted.

To believe that everything just happens is the same as a farmer believing that apples will grow up in his garden without the planting of the seed. Anger doesn't just show up; thoughts of a suffered wrong caused it to show up. Depression doesn't just appear; you think unpleasant thoughts first. Jealousy doesn't just arrive; thoughts in fear of not having or being without are present first. Your possessions didn't just appear on your doorstep one morning; you thought your possessions into existence through believing along with practical applications to obtain it. You farmed it. We farm everything. If you trace your beliefs back to its starting points, you will find that the words that were spoken to you from childhood to adulthood were the seeds responsible for the acceptance and the nurturing of your current beliefs today.

We have come to learn that there is one higher than ourselves that is responsible for all creation in whose hands the entire universe thrives. What we have been lacking in our knowledge is two things: that the book of instruction pertaining to human life and how it is to be lived is the Holy Bible, and that it is pertaining to the here and now, it says very little about heaven. Our victories as well as our failures are within these few scriptures:

The power of life and death are in the tongue and those who love it will eat its fruit.

From the fruit of his lips a man enjoys good things but the unfaithful have a craving for violence. He who guards his lips guards his life but he who speaks rashly will come to ruin.

—Proverbs 13:2-3

Since they hated knowledge and did not choose to fear the Lord, since they would not accept my advice and spurned my rebuke, they will eat the fruit of their ways and be filled with the fruit of their schemes.

—Proverbs 29:31

Whoever would love life and see good days must keep his tongue from evil and his lips from deceitful speech, for the eyes of the Lord are on the righteous and his ears are attentive to their prayer, but the face of the Lord is against those who do evil.

—1 Peter 3:10

There are countless scriptures that give clear instructions for life and how to live it purposefully and successfully. But in our minds clouded by ignorance due to sin: hatred, anger, jealousy, drunkenness, idolatry, sexual immorality, murder, envy, strife, and the lack of temperance, we became oblivious to the fact that in these things we are rich, but when it comes to the things of God: Love, joy, peace, patience, forgiveness and faith, just to name a few, we remain poor. Living in total darkness, one is led to believe that he can still live a good life living within in the lower realm of life so long as he masters the thing in which he strives for which will ultimately bring him wealth. For this reason, many are destroyed by their wealth due to their lack of knowledge in regards to its source.

The seedtime and harvest law allows us to share in the power of God. It was intended for our good, to be fruitful in everything we do. But when sin entered the world through the master of defeat, (Satan) he took full advantage of this infallible law that god has sent forth into the earth and so now he uses it fully to his advantage afforded through the opportunity our sin provided.

If the seeds we sow are for the common good, God will nurture them and the fruit thereof will be of great benefit to you and others. However, on the other hand, if the seeds sown are of ill will, Satan is summoned to govern that seed and its fruit will be to your own destruction.

Through our will to do and the law of God, the harvest we produce in our lives will be the determining factor of whom we have made lord over our life in this earth.

In this law, you will find the cause behind every kind of destruction and in this same law; you will find the remedy for peace, health, and wealth. For if man is condemned by his own ignorance, he is also restored by his knowledge.

By this law, a person can consciously create their life's events and circumstances in advance by faith in having the things desired by a conscious, constructive, purposeful mind-set, so long as the motive is love.

Seedtime and harvest is the overall conclusion to all things that ever existed in life. In this law, you will find the beginning and the end, the problem and the solution, the cause and the effect to most every situation. This truth is demonstrated and reported throughout the history of the Bible from Adam's fall to the ministry of Jesus. It is the focus of every study in medicine, science, philosophy, and religion all conclusively resting in harmony by this law.

For centuries spiritual pioneers have built their ministries based on this law, and it is still being preached throughout the world today by the Christian ministry leaders. Even spiritual teachers of no specific faith have submitted themselves to this truth and are reaping great benefits from it, and everyone that is consciously exposed to this truth is hungry for the wisdom, power, and the administration of this law in hopes to better their lives.

The wisdom and power this law provides is beyond any human comprehension and is difficult for the carnal mind to comprehend, but is very real and extremely beneficial for those who are willing to consciously apply the spiritual and practical principles that governs this law to their lives.

Jesus gave many illustrations in parables regarding this law and compared its administration to the administration of God's kingdom and its operation.

In doing so, he concluded that this kingdom is within every believer.

> *Once, having been asked by the Pharisees when the kingdom of God would come, Jesus replied, "The kingdom of God does not come with your careful observation, nor will people say, 'Here it is,' or 'There it is,' because the kingdom of God is within you."*
> —Luke 17:20-21

Consciously or subconsciously, we were created to live by this law, and so we do. The problem has always been our lack of knowledge. We were never taught that spiritual development is vital for life in order to live it effectively, according to how God has designed it. We were never taught about seedtime and harvest, cause and effect, reaping and sowing, yet these phrases have been mentioned to us all by one person or another during our lifetime, but they remained empty, with no real understanding behind them unless we were given the opportunity to apply them to someone else's life, only then was this law apparent.

Many of us were raised to deal with the effects of life, and by doing so, we have become oblivious to the cause of life. But if we can start here and begin to accept our role in the circumstances in which we have been living, change can now run its course. But we have to be willing to face some very hurtful truths about ourselves, and with this conviction, restoration can begin. There is a reason for everything; nothing just happens. The question is; are you willing to listen?

Chapter 1

The Kingdom of God

Once having been asked by the Pharisees when the kingdom of God will come, Jesus replied, "the kingdom of God does not come with your careful observation, nor will people say 'here it is,' or 'there it is,' because the kingdom of God is within you."

—Luke 17: 21-21

The knowledge of the secrets of the kingdom of heaven has been given to you, but not to them. Whoever has will be given more, and he will have an abundance. Whoever does not have, even what he has will be taken from him.

—Matthew 13:11-12

The kingdom of God has been given to all who are in Christ. Its the secret wisdom of God in regards to life and how it ought to be lived in accordance with the spiritual principles that have been established for our benefit. In this kingdom, one will find the wisdom for everlasting peace, love, strength, health, and wealth, that can only be truly received through the revealed knowledge of God.

> *If any of you lacks wisdom, he should ask God, who gives generously to all without finding fault, and it will be given to him.*
>
> —James 1:5

This kingdom has righteousness as its foundation and is governed by spiritual principles that God has established before creation. When these principles are applied through faith, they bring about conditions in life that far exceeds what we are capable of achieving through our own human efforts. Through this kingdom, health is restored, true wealth is gained, and God's will prevails as the fruits of righteousness are developed and administered according to God's purpose.

> *The secret of the kingdom of God has been given to you. But those outside, everything is said in parables.*
>
> —Mark 4:11

It is, in truth, a recipe for all of life's functions and a remedy to all of life's malfunctions. It's God's way of operation, his divine order of life. It's his word being established and demonstrated in all of nature, also in the human heart, governed by seedtime and harvest, reaping and sowing. It's the ripened fruit of his word being manifested in the life of the believer, the man who lives his life in *full power* according to the *seedtime and harvest* law.

> *What shall we say the kingdom of God is like or what parable shall we use to describe it. It is like a mustard seed which is the smallest seed you plant in the ground. Yet when planted, it grows and becomes the largest of all garden plants, with such big branches that the birds of the air can perch in its shade.*
>
> —Mark 4:30-32

As a farmer sows an apple seed into the earth expecting to receive an abundance of apples, so it is also with the human heart. A man plants seeds of love into the human heart, and so he becomes a vessel of love, expressing that love toward others through words and acts of kindness, patience, and forgiveness, and in doing so, he receives love in return. In light of this spiritual law of return, a man may plant seeds of evil into the human heart, and by the law of return as we see in all living things, when the evil seed is ripened, evil is expressed through his words, acts, and deeds, and by this, he becomes a vessel of evil, expresses his evil into the lives of others through slander, hate, unforgiveness, irritability, and the like, and he receives in return slander, hate and unforgiveness, and irritability from others.

You brood of vipers, how can you who are evil say anything good? For out of the overflow of the heart the mouth speaks. The good man brings good things out of the good stored up in him, and the evil man brings evil things out of the evil stored up in him.

—Mark 12:34-35

The kingdom of God in its simplest expression is "knowledge and power." Knowledge to do and power to give and receive all good things life has to offer. Satan also has a kingdom, and those who willfully or blindly live their lives in a selfish state of mind is under satanic control because selfishness is the root of all human suffering, and by this, he has separated himself from the things of God.

The difference between the one who has inherited the kingdom of God and those who have not is this: the one who has inherited the kingdom has earned the keys to its secret wisdom of operation by the purification of his heart in true repentance.

He has realized that all human suffering derives from the fruits of selfishness, which are rage, greed, adultery, fornication, perversion, anger, strife, bitterness, unforgiveness, idolatry, murder, slander, gluttony, addiction, and every other kind of evil, and having come to this truth, he has found that all these evils develop in the human heart first before they are given to the world in the form of suffering.

He has taken the searchlight of purity, love, compassion, peace, and patience and set its beam of light on the elements of his own heart in search of error, and in doing so, he has humbled himself, having found the cause of his own suffering by identifying himself with the evils of the world.

Now having located its source, his spirit now rises to the surface and demands freedom and redemption from its current state of death. As he aspires toward a life of heavenly virtue through purification and walking through what he now considers to be the pit of hell on earth, in long-suffering, patience, determination, and faith, he has arrived at a life of blessedness as he becomes a vessel of love, peace, righteousness, and power. All of life becomes clear to him, and he now realizes that all forms of creation live by the same spiritual principle: *seedtime and harvest*. He has come to understand that just as he had once planted seeds of evil and got evil in return, he can now commence to planting seeds of good, and by doing so, he will enter into a life of blessedness. To him, life has become as simple as the simplest mathematical equation. His spiritual eyes have been opened.

As for the man outside of the kingdom, he continues to live in the sins of the world and is content in doing so. He believes that he can sow evil and gather the good because instant self gratification is his aim in life therefore, he fails to recognize the source of his troubles. He believes he has life in the palm of his hands by manipulating circumstances, people, and things in order to satisfy his beastly appetite. He lives according to what his flesh desires now and answers its every call. Being led by his sinful nature, better known as 'the flesh', he is spiritually dead therefore, he lacks spiritual discernment. He sees others as being the source of his pain, anger, rage, and irritability. In this state of mind, he says to himself and others, "I'm not an angry person, people provoke me into it." He owns up to none of his ways and justifies his every evil reaction by the action of others.

Cause and effect, action and reaction, reaping and sowing are complicated subjects to this unenlightened mind, and as for him in his life, one has nothing to do with the other, although he is happy to relate this law of karma to the affliction of others.

He justifies his shortcomings by his environment and current circumstances. To him, life is very complicated and every undesirable circumstance that he has found himself facing, in his eyes, comes to him by default. He lives in the luck system, therefore everything good or bad happens by luck or association.

Although the secret wisdom of life is located in the tree growing in his own backyard, he is blinded to its wisdom by his own ego swallowed up in ignorance.

Because of this, he has separated himself from the eternal good in life by storing up for himself the riches of this world. Yea, he has become rich in every kind of evil. But to him, living in darkness, indulging in every kind of sin, he has not considered the wages of sin or the cost of his actions; therefore, he knows not why he stumbles. As long as love, purity, forgiveness, peace, and compassion remain foolish to him, he will remain in darkness. Unless he humbles himself, realizing that he is in need of a savior, he will continue to be a prisoner of darkness and the redemption of his soul is denied.

The law of seedtime and harvest may be unrealistic to most people and too complicated to discern, but the truth will remain the truth, and nothing in this life can change the spiritual laws of which we live by. It will be what it shall be.

Chapter 2

Light on the Material World

Do not love the world or anything in the world. If anyone loves the world, the love of the Father is not in him. For everything in the world—the cravings of sinful man, the lust of his eyes and the boasting of what he has and does—comes not from the Father but from the world. The world and its desires pass away, but the man who does the will of God lives forever.

—1 John 2:15-17

The material mind has formed its way of thinking from the material world, the world we have created for ourselves through creative thinking. Our material mind is made up of falsehood, impure thoughts that do not line up with the word of God or his will for our lives.

This mind-set is called the inferior mind. This is because it opposes the truth and offers falsehood in every sense and operates against the way God has designed us to think, feel, and speak.

The material mind has its mind-set on what it can see and feel and is governed by outward effects only. It judges everything based on its five physical senses and has no working knowledge of the spirit within. It causes us to put all our hope into what is seen rather than what's not, and when our life becomes undesirable, we try to change what's already been established, by physical means using physical resources to change or recreate the thing that was brought forth and created in the spiritual realm to begin with. But what we have failed to realize is that everything that exists is the effect of a cause and therefore becomes a *dead effect* once created. This means; when something is created in the mind and brought into physical form by faith and actions, it has already at that point, reached it's full potential of existence.

Now in light of this truth, when it comes down to diseases, mental conditions or environmental effects, those are also considered to be dead effects. The disease was brought to life by faith in their ability to destroy you and so they take their form in the members of one's body becoming a physical condition with a mission. As for the environmental effects; they are already created conditions. *Proverbs 10: 15* states that *"poverty is the ruin of the poor"*, translated; poverty is the result of the poor in spirit. Poverty is a mind set that is brought to life through hopelessness and faith in its ability to overtake you and so it does.

Now, the difference between a physical thing vs. a physical condition is; the material thing can be destroyed by your hands and the other can be destroyed by faith in your ability to overcome it. However, they are both a by-product of your mind and since you have been given the ability to choose what you think, change can now run its course. So in order to change the effect, we must start at the cause. The cause lies within you, in what you have accepted as truth.

But it has not always been this way. The material mind has been bent into its former way of thinking. I use the word *bent* because that is not the way our mind was created to think. The material mind says these things to you: because cancer, diabetes, high blood pressure, and alcoholism runs in your family, chances are, you will get it also. Once an addict, always an addict. It tells you to accept the lower standards of life set for us by our community, parents, and the environment in which we were raised in with its opinions, beliefs, and prejudices.

It tells us we are our parents, whether it's born to poverty, obesity, drugs, alcohol, temperament, even teenage childbearing. Now because all of those things lead to destruction, we can safely say that they are impure, and they have formed seats of habit grounded in our subconscious mind. As we move along in life, it attracts to itself similar thoughts for its development until one day-your beliefs return to you as a full manifested condition. All you have to do is see it and accept it to be a possibility for you, and it's done for you. Your impure thoughts have the power to shut down the original purpose for your life.

Chapter 3

Creative Power

> *The Lord God formed the man from the dust of the ground and breathed into his nostrils the breath of life, and the man became a living soul.*
>
> —Genesis 2:7

> *What the wicked dreads will overtake him, what the righteous desire will be granted.*
>
> —Proverbs 10:24

Mankind was created to live by thought. In fact, in our true nature, we should be referred to as *thought beings* instead of human beings. In error, we have been taught to live according to our human nature, and so our logic for every kind of failure or undesired circumstance is "we're only human." But it is this kind of mind-set that is responsible for every failure that we endure in life. Referring to ourselves as *only human* is a false sense of contentment suggested by Satan, which is, in fact, an empowerment to fail. This label gives us a license to fail. This rule tells us that we are weak in our own true nature, therefore, unequipped to overcome adversities, that things just happen. They come to us beyond our control, by default; therefore, we are powerless to control them, nor do we have the ability to turn situations around in the nature of which we boast our so-called human nature. This perception would be true if we were in fact, 'only human'. But we're not. We have three natures, (spirit, soul, body). The human nature refers to the body and the physical sense that it was created with.

So in this mind-set, we develop a failure mentality, and it is because of this perception many accept failure and are defeated at almost every turn.

His divine power has given us everything we need for life and godliness <u>through our knowledge</u> of him who called us by his own glory and goodness. Through these he has given us his very great and precious promises, so that through them you may participate in the <u>divine nature</u> and escape the corruption in the world caused by evil desires.

—2 Peter 1:3-4

This scripture teaches us that we become empowered through our knowledge of God, of whom he created us to be *in him*, made in his likeness, therefore, able to participate in his divine nature. His nature is within his power or ability to create and control. Being made in his likeness, we also have the same creative ability within ourselves. But if we are to ever tap into this power that our Creator has created in us, we must first begin to understand who we are and closely examine the three natures in which we were created with: spirit, soul, and body.

> *The Lord God formed the man from the dust of the ground and breathed into his nostrils the breath of life, and the man became a living soul.*
>
> —Genesis 2:7

We refer to God as the Holy Trinity: Father, Son, Holy Spirit. Well, being made in his image and likeness, we also have three natures that we live by: spirit, soul, body. Allow me to explain to you your extraordinary nature.

The Bible says when God breathed into the nostrils of Adam, he breathed into him his spirit, which is the spirit of life. It was then that he became a living soul.

Our bodies are just a tool in which our spirit and soul uses to express itself, and the soul is a counterpart of our human nature in addition to our spirit. Allow me to elaborate on how wonderfully we were created.

The physical body was created to relate and participate in the creation of the physical environment of which he created for us; therefore, our physical nature can only relate to the things of this physical world. Therefore, when people perceive themselves as being 'only human', and this world being in the destructive state that its in, they can only measure life in accordance with what they see happening in the world. And its because of their limited ability to see themselves as a more valuable asset created in the likeness of their creator that they are deceived therefore destroyed.

The human spirit was given to man to relate to the things of God, giving us the ability to participate in his creative nature by creating a physical environment around us in accordance to our needs as he has created the heavenly realms for himself. Its the power to bring our desires into existence through faith in our ability to obtain them. Look around you, all that man has ever created, obtained or achieved started with faith in their ability to do so. The soul is the middle man and has the ability to relate to both spiritual and physical sides of life. It's a direct connection between God and man. It's who we are all wrapped up in one and will be the determining factor of where we end up in life.

Like the Holy Trinity and the three natures of which we were created with, the soul also has three natures within itself: mind, will, and emotions. Within these three are the origin for all life's occurrences; it's the heart of life. Now the soul has very fascinating and intricate abilities, and within itself, there's great power. With this knowledge, you will discover not only the cause behind every evil thing established here on earth, but you will also come to the full knowledge of restoration with power to change any undesired thing that your soul has established for you.

With this objective in mind, let us begin to examine a counterpart of the soul, the mind of a man. Our mind is the storehouse of our thoughts. It's where all of the things we have ever believed in faith or fear are hidden. It's where our thoughts begin and are processed for future manifestation. The human mind was created with a correspondent nature called the image-maker better known as the imagination, which reflects back to us in picture form, our thoughts and our words. By this spiritual process, we are able to see what the naked eye cannot see. The birth of all of our hopes, dreams, and despair are contingent upon this process and is reflected back to us in images, and it is because of these images we either aspire to come up higher or fall into hopelessness. What one sees with his natural eyes are meaningless because they reflect what's already in the world, brought into manifestation through someone else's ability to create, limiting us in regard to what we can or cannot obtain. But our third eye, called the imagination, is able to see greater things beyond the limits this world has set for us. It guides us by helping us contribute to the world the things we see in our minds as a possibility or reality, and it's because of our imagination the world continues to advance beyond limitation therefore, there are no limits. With that being said, the only value our natural eyes can have is the ability to keep us from falling and bumping into walls since what we want out of life is not subjected to the conditions of this world.

Think of your spirit as a manufacturing center. It plays a vital role in regard to the life we live. As a farmer plants a seed into the soil of the earth to bring forth fruit, in the same way the spirit is likened to that soil. It's the core essence of our life. Because of it, we live, breathe, and exist; without it, we die and our bodies fall straight to the ground. As the soil comes before the seed, the spirit also comes before life. As the elements of the soil adds its life-giving substance to the seed planted in order to bring forth fruitage of that seed, the same thing is true in regard to our spirit; it adds its life-giving substance to our body to bring forth our life. But it doesn't stop there; it's also the source of all created things. Our spirit develops whatever has been dropped into it by our soul; therefore, our soul is responsible for the condition of the human spirit.

Because our mind is part of our soul, whatever conditions we accept mentally are dropped into our spirit as seeds for its development, and so we become a by-product of our thoughts. If thoughts of evil are dropped into your spirit, then anger, strife, malice will be expressed by you to the world. If seeds of love are dropped into our spirit by our thoughts, we express this same love into the world through channels of forgiveness, patients, acceptance and appreciation. In light of this process, it becomes clear that our actions are nothing more than the vessels in which the ripened fruit of our thoughts are carried into the world as a knock on someone's door. By this spiritual process, our contribution to the world is deposited into the hearts of those who are most receptive to receive it.

It is therefore safe to conclude that if there is any harm done, it is not within the action itself that produced it or any other physical thing we consider to be evil but within the thought that produced it and brought it to life because had it not been for the thought, manifestation of any kind would be impossible.

> *Whenever one comes to see me, he speaks falsely, while his heart gathers slander; then he goes out and spreads it abroad.*
>
> —Psalms 41:6

In light of this truth, we can safely say that everything that reaches full expression was first created in a thought. And if this is true, and it is, then we have now located the power to change our circumstances altogether. Our freedom is located within this truth. Rejecting this truth means all the good in life is lost, including your life. It means your purpose in this present earth is to suffer defeat. It means you have no savior. Jesus came to this physical planet not only to bring salvation, but also to save our souls in hopes to deliver our physical bodies from its present condition corrupted by sin.

> *Later Jesus found him at the temple and said to him, "See, you are well again. Stop sinning or something worse may happen to you." The man went away and told the Jews that it was Jesus who had made him well.*
>
> —John 5:14-15

Chapter 4

Light on Love and Fear

This grace was given me: to preach to all people the unsearchable riches of Christ, and to make plain to everyone the administration of this mystery, which for ages past was kept hidden in God who created all things.

—Ephesians 3:8

If I speak in the tongues of men and of angels, but have not love, I am only a resounding gong or a clanging cymbal. If I have the gift of prophecy and can fathom all mysteries and all knowledge, and if I have a faith that can move mountains, but have not love, I am nothing. If I give all I possess to the poor and surrender my body to the flames, but have not love, I gain nothing.

—1 Corinthians 13:1-3

And now these three remain: faith, hope and love. But the greatest of these is love.

—1 Corinthians 13:13

By these scriptures, we know that love is the key to all the good things of God. Many of us were raised to have more faith in the things we fear, the problems of this world, things we can see. The problem with this kind of up bringing is that it has for generations failed us due to the lack of spiritual truth behind it. Therefore, what was good for us one year became hazardous to our health in the next. We have put our faith in what mankind said was good, but when it failed, fear entered through the effects and testimonies of other people and as a direct result, fear cancelled out our faith.

Do not call conspiracy everything that these people call conspiracy; do not fear what they fear, and do not dread it.

—Isaiah 8:12

Fear finds its origin in Satan's distribution center. It's manufactured as a copy of faith because the feelings and symptoms that accompany it seem more real than our faith in time of great distress. His mission is to take the things of God and make it his own by manipulating our belief system. Faith and love is the foundation of God's kingdom, Satan's copies the two by building his kingdom on fear and hate, which can appear to be just as powerful and real on the surface of our flesh. Oblivious of our true nature and the victory we have in our Savior, we expect and accept life at its worst. Satan is well aware of the power we have in Christ through faith and has implemented fear by manipulating our physical senses to overpower our faith in order to achieve his goal which is defeat. Again, we were all born into a broken world, a world that is in distress by the effects of sin. At every turn, we see human destruction, and since our physical nature can only relate to this physical world, oblivious of our spiritual strength, we become one with the conditions around us. Satan is well aware of our weak physical nature, and so he uses it to his glory afforded by our ignorance.

> *There is no fear in love. But perfect love drives out fear, because fear has to do with punishment. The one who fears is not made perfect in love.*
>
> —1 John 4:18

Faith is a spiritual principle used to govern and produce everything in this natural world including evil schemes. But its original purpose was to empower those who are in Christ Jesus to overcome the destruction this world provides. But the law of faith does not cease due to your unbelief. It's eternal and comes from the eternal nature of God. It is a gift intended for our benefit, not our destruction. However, faith when appropriated in fear will produce fearlike conditions. Faith is likened to water. Just as water is a natural substance that governs the growth and vitality of all living things, so it is with our faith. It's a spiritual substance used to govern all spiritual things that are brought into existence.

Love, joy, peace, happiness, laughter, forgiveness and compassion are all spiritual components of love because although we cannot see them, we can feel the effects of them in our natural body. These effects lead to long life. The same thing is true where fear is concerned. Anger, jealousy, sorrow, defeat, rage, and heartache are all counter parts of fear, and these spiritual conditions wage war against the members of our body by creating stresslike conditions, which will lead to stress related conditions, resulting in premature death. The point to take is none of these thoughts can be seen, yet they all exist by reaching a form of expression in our feelings by the law of growth, which produces an atmosphere of its kind. Therefore whatever feeling are within us, belong to us and so they its conditions become one with us.

Our world functions in the law of growth, and the law of growth is governed by the spirit of love. The law of growth ceases by the law of fear because fear brings torment and premature death to all things. For example, a good idea dies at the brink of fear. It will keep it from coming to life. Good health is jeopardized at the thought of fear. The body responds to the conditions of our mind, so when we fear something, it creates a stressful atmosphere within our bodies causing our organs to work harder than they were created to; therefore, premature death is summoned.

Whatever is entertained in the mind, whether it is good or bad has a need for expression. The ground (your spirit) is no respecter of seed; it doesn't know whether the seeds you sow are good or bad, it only knows to grow what's been planted, your most dominant thoughts. Either way, it returns back to you in physical form manifested from your thoughts. It's the divine order of life. Our life changes as we grow and mature, and the things we acquire along the way are contingent upon our previous mind-set.

Every living thing grows, and everything that has life started with some kind of seed, be it physical seeds or *word seeds*. Many of us ignore the cause and deal with the effects only. If we could ever hope to change any undesired effect in our life, we have to deal with the root, the cause. Since the situation that presented itself is only the physical material of the hidden truth, it would be pointless to change our acts alone. But to change our actions does have some spiritual value. When a person desires to change their ways, they starts by breaking the habit of doing it. Constant repetition formed the habit; therefore, it will take constant repetition of not doing to break it. But understand that this is only dealing with the surface of the situation. If one does not attempt to change his thinking, which is the root of poverty, anger, jealousy, discord, hate, malice, unforgiveness, and so on, his actions will bring into manifestation the ripened fruit which is certain to cause conflict, not only to others but mainly to himself. In fact, it will bring more harm to the person who distributes it because the law of return guarantees what belongs to you will certainly return to you, be it love or hate, a hundredfold. Then we scream out in despair, "Why is this happening to me?"

Mind over matter is the key principle that governs life. Seedtime and harvest is the secret administration in Gods kingdom.

> *This is what the kingdom of God is like. A man scatters seed on the ground. Night and day, whether he sleeps or gets up, the seed sprouts and grows, though he does not know how. All by itself the "soil" produces grain.*
> —Mark 4:26-28

This law of growth was not only applied to natural farming, Jesus particularly referred to *seed* as being *thoughts* and *words*.

Chapter 5

Light on the Blessed Life

There are many people who will say that they are blessed while living in poverty, discord, and disease in which all is found in the spirit of darkness governed by Satan himself.

They have no true peace in their life and so choose to live in harmony with their circumstances by clothing their discord with contentment. I must admit that is a brighter way of looking at hopelessness. But to truly be content means to have peace in all areas of life by declaring victory in every battle. Its within our victories we find peace. In such contentment, affliction cannot remain.

Some proclaim in light of God giving them another day is a blessing in itself and is all the blessing they need from God. That mind-set is not incorrect but incomplete. But try convincing a starving, dying child that he is blessed to look forward to another day of hunger. Consider the terminally ill patients in the hospitals around the world that are in morbid pain, then put yourself in their shoes and see how it would feel to look forward to another day of this *limited version* of the blessing.

There are many more situations in which people feel there is no hope, and for them life might as well be over. For what good is life if one has no purpose or hope of a better day, a future without pain and suffering in this present earth as we know it.

How could a blessing so limited to just breathing benefit our lives or the lives of others for that matter? If we all had to look forward to hopelessness, disease, and unnatural death, there would be no happiness or success; in fact mankind would have no purpose, much less serve a purpose. We would then have no other alternative but to conclude that the life God has created for us is nothing more than a tease and a cruel joke. Our lives would be a living hell with more hell to look forward to when we die because hopelessness is based in fear, and fear is governed by Satan who is rooted and grounded in sin, who will lead us into wickedness due to our hopelessness resulting in self-preservation and destruction.

The same thing is true with faith. Christ is the developer and lord over our faith. Faith *gives life*, fear *takes lives*.

So then I ask you, how can you be fully blessed not being able to provide for your children? Does it go well with you to have them go out into this world on their own, fearful, dreadful, hopeless, confused, and oblivious to the power of faith and blessings and expect them to be all they can be? How can they when they live in a generational curse of lack and limitation set off by us as parents who have demonstrated a false idea of faith and blessings?

To be blessed is to be empowered to succeed, to overcome darkness, and to have peace in every arena of life. To be "more than a conqueror" is being able overcome adversity and life's challenges through the power of God that is at work within us.

This means that we have been given liberty to use our supernatural strength that God has given us through his spirit, which is activated by our faith in it to have *victory over* the circumstances that sets itself up against us, to come out of it *ahead*. I'm not implying that life should be an easy road and by having faith, nothing can ever happen to us. Life in all its ways will challenge us because we have been born into a world of sin and sin brings destruction, but this is what God has to say about our adversities.

A thousand may fall at your side and ten thousand at your right hand, <u>but it will not come near</u>

you. You will only observe with your eyes and see the punishment of the wicked. If you make the most high your dwelling—even the Lord (Jesus), who is my refuge—then no harm will befall you, no disaster will come near your tent. For he will command his angels concerning you, to keep you in all your ways. They will lift you up in their hands so that you will not strike your foot on a stone. You will tread upon a lion and the cobra, you will trample the great lion and the serpent . . . "because he loves me" says the Lord, I will rescue him. I will protect him, for he acknowledges my name. He will call upon me and I will answer him; I will be with him in trouble, I will deliver him and honor him. With long life will I satisfy him and show him my salvation.

—Psalm 91:7-14

Salvation in this life means a saving of somebody from harm, destruction, difficulty, failure, and death.

Who is he that condemns us? Jesus Christ who died—more than that, was raised to life—is at the right hand of God, interceding for us. Shall trouble or hardship, or persecution or famine, or nakedness or danger or sword? For your sake we face death all day long: we are considered (by Satan) as sheep to be slaughtered. No, in all these things, we are "more than conquers through him who loves us."

—Romans 8:34

These scriptures among many others signify the magnitude of God's love and the blessing in operation to bring us peace and victory in everything. This blessing has no limits. This is the limitless word of God in which brings us hope, freedom, peace, and life in all its abundance. This is the armor of which our children should have in order to face the unpredictable world in which we live in.

Finally, be strong in the Lord and in his mighty power. Put on the full armor of God so that you can take your stand against the devils schemes. For our struggle is not against flesh and bone, but against the powers of this dark world and the spiritual forces of evil. Therefore, put on the full armor of God, so that <u>when</u> the day of evil comes, you may be able to stand your ground, and after you have done everything to stand. Stand firm then with the belt of truth buckled around your waist, with the breastplate of righteousness in place, and with your feet fitted with the readiness that comes from the gospel of peace. In addition to all this, take up the shield of faith with which you can extinguish all the flaming arrows *from the evil one. Take the helmet of salvation and the sword of the spirit which is the word of God and pray in the spirit, on all occasions with all kinds of request.*

—Ephesians 6:10-18

This is the protection in which the blessing provides. This is the gospel of *peace* in which Jesus preached and formed his ministry. His ministry was based on faith in the word of the living God. His administration of healing the sick, raising the dead, feeding the poor, casting out demons, making a way out of no way, turning little of nothing into plenty of something, having all that he needed for himself and thousands of others, all these miracles were demonstrated through the power of faith. We have all been given the measure of faith with the same ability.

I tell you the truth, anyone who has faith in me <u>will do what I have been doing. He will do even greater things than these</u> because I am going to my father, I will do whatever you ask in my name so that I may bring glory to my father.

—John 14:12

This particular scripture should be a clear indication of God's will for our lives. All that Jesus has done was for the glory of God. During his healing ministry, he never once considered a person's race or religious beliefs. He condemned no one, no matter what their sin was. He healed all and fed all and confirmed that by faith, we can walk as he walked and do all that he has done through the power of God that's at work within us through the Holy Spirit. This is the glory and will of God for us, and it's taking place right now.

Through this we know that to walk in the blessing (*power*) of the almighty God is to walk in his total protection at all times, that if we pray according to his will, all our prayers will be answered, and that the limited version of the blessing (just being alive and barely making it) is only a false sense of hope the devil uses as a tool to entice us into false contentment, which leaves us powerless and receptive to the will and the way of the enemy. It maliciously guides us into poverty, disease, unhappiness, discord, and accepting the *unnatural death syndrome* by our own will. In doing so, we become one with the evil one, just as the righteous becomes one with the one who is righteous. The Bible says that it's impossible to please God without faith, and those who don't believe his word has a wicked heart of darkness.

Why is my language not clear to you? It's because you are unable to hear what I say . . . you belong to your father the devil and you want to carry out your father's desires. He was a murderer from the beginning, there is no truth in him, for he is a liar and the father of lies, yet because I tell the truth, you cannot hear me. He who belongs to God hears what God says.

—John 8:43

If our faith is not rooted in the word of God, how then can we walk in his divine protection? Such a person is incapable of receiving the fullness of his grace. Those who choose to reject the blessings God has given us in his promises will continue to live their natural life under the curse and destruction of Satan.

This day I call heaven and earth as witnesses against you that I have set before you life and death, blessings and curses. Choose life so that you and your children may live.

—Deuteronomy 30:19

I'm not implying that this person's eternal salvation is based on whether or not he or she is able to receive the blessings of God. Eternal salvation comes by grace through faith in what God has accomplished through Christ completely void of our religious acts of worship.

> *For it is by grace you have been saved through faith—and this not of yourselves, it is the gift of God.*
> —Ephesians 2:8

However, there is another salvation of which Christ has brought with him, and this is the salvation of our natural bodies. Salvation means to be saved, delivered, or rescued from a thing, and Christ demonstrated this physical salvation through his healing ministry, and it also is received by faith in his ability to restore us through his spirit. It empowers us to overcome any challenge or stronghold that we may face with victory. To reject it will cause our hardships to overtake us physically but not spiritually.

To be blessed means to be empowered by the spirit of God to draw to you those things that are needed or desired in accordance with God's will. That's how the Bible interprets the blessing. We can say we're blessed until the cows come home, but if we're not living it, taking it by faith, we will never walk in it. It's like leaving a harvest in the field to rot. You see it in your own front yard, but you choose not to believe it was put there for you. You have faith in it but can't see God giving it to you. We will all have to answer to God for our selfishness and unbelief because that harvest was not put there for our sake alone, but for the sake of others.

We are responsible for our children's well-being and mind-set for generations to come, passing on spiritual guidance and blessing just as the leaders of the Bible have done with their families. This does not mean that we are to take on the burden of financial security and distribution for generations to come, for money is not the source of power. Power remains in your ability to farm it through the spiritual principles that God has established through seedtime and harvest, the law of return. What I am saying is we can have all the money in the world, but if we lack power and spiritual guidance, not only do we destroy ourselves, but we destroy our children.

The point to take is God has given us the power to obtain health, wealth, and peace, and we also have the power to administer the source of these blessings to the lives of our children. Our children should never want for any good thing such food and health along with the normal things desired to live comfortably as a young adult. But if we can equip them to walk in the power of faith as they witness it operating in our own lives, they shall also never be without, always being able to provide for themselves and others through the power of the blessing that they witnessed operating within their home. And they will in turn provide their children with the same weapons for spiritual warfare. Becoming "more than conquerors," living under the blessing, not the curse.

All the great leaders of the Bible walked by faith and were restored in every area of their life although some chose to accept conviction and persecution as their spiritual act of worship just as Jesus did. God spoke to them and told them what to do in order to have what they had. You may view the leaders of the Bible as being poor. They were leaders of countrysides (which are now nations in our time), and power was their wealth. They owned all things worth owning from cattle and gold to power, having and supplying all that was needed for them and their followers, and their faith and obedience got it to them. They had the power to pass on their blessings. So when their children received the blessing by faith and were sent out into the world alone, they left with only cattle to trade and offer to God but power through the blessing became their shield. The blessing was powerful and effective in the lives of all the great leaders and their time.

Look at Cain and Abel; the first murder in history took place because one brother presented a better offering to God than the other and received the blessing.

It is not through the law that Abraham and his offsprings received the promise that he would be heir to the world, but through the righteousness that comes by faith.

—Romans 4:13-14

Verses 16-17 goes on to explain:

Therefore the promise comes by faith, and that it may be by grace and may be guaranteed to all Abrahams off springs, not only to those who are of the law,(Jews) but also to those who are of the faith of Abraham. He is the father if us all. As it is written: "I have made you father of many nations." He is our father in the sight of God, in whom he believed—the God who gives life to the dead and calls things that are not as though they were.

Verse 18 continues,

Against all hope, Abraham in hope believed and so became the father of many nations, just as it had been said to him, "so shall your seed be." Without weakening in his faith, he knew he was as good as dead through old age. Yet he did not waver through unbelief regarding the promise of God, but was strengthened in his faith giving glory to God, being fully persuaded God had the power to do what he had promised him.

The story of Joseph is yet another inspiring story of the blessing. God appeared to Joseph in a dream and told him that he would be a leader and all his older brothers would bow down to him. Due to their wickedness, the blessing was passed to Joseph. Out of jealousy, they tried to destroy him in his blessing by torturing him and sold him as a slave to the Egyptians. While a slave, he was favored and put in charge of the pharaoh's jail in which he dwelled. This was due to the blessing. He was also dressed in the finest of cloths and put in charge of Potiphar's house while still a slave. This proves the blessing was still at work even in captivity. Later he was made to be governor of all of Egypt. During his adversity as a slave, Joseph held true to God's promise of leadership, and it was brought to pass just as God promised. All the favors Joseph experienced as a slave was no surprise to him, for he knew what it meant to be blessed.

You are from God and have overcome them because the one in you is greater than the one in the world.

—1 John 4:14

Jesus said that we are saved by faith, in other words, we can be delivered from anything if we dare to believe. And faith is "being sure of what we hope for, and certain of what's to come," knowing that you have it when you've asked, even if it is not yet a manifested fact but believing that God's promise will bring it to pass in due time. Holy scripture tells us that faith without deeds is dead:

> *As the body without the spirit is dead, so faith without deeds is dead.*
>
> —James 2:26)

The Bible is full of promises for all things pertaining to life and godliness through the knowledge of him.

> *Do not waste time arguing over godless ideas and old wives' tales. Instead, train yourself to be godly. Physical training is good, but training for godliness is much better, promising benefits in this life and in the life to come.*
>
> —1 Timothy 4:7-8

Keep one thing in mind; your faith does not move God, your faith is a positive response to what God has already done. Our only job is to become acquainted with what he has already provided for us, accept them to be true for us, and to stand on it by faith. The promise is a seed, and we are to water it with God's words until it becomes a living reality as we subconsciously do in all things that are brought into existence.

Knowledge is dead without the application of the primary principle. You may have read the Bible and you may very well be able to quote it by memory. But if you fail to apply to your life what you've learned, you will never benefit from it. As holy scripture teaches us,

> *My son, pay attention to what I say, listen closely to my words. Do not let them out of your sight, keep them within your heart; for they are life to those who find them and health to a man's whole body. Above all else, guard your heart for it is the wellspring of life.*

We are to plant God's promises in the garden of our hearts. Saying is sowing, and your heart is the ground in which the seed will grow. Jesus also explains and demonstrates this truth in Matthew 13, the parable of the sower, Mark 4:13, and in Luke 8:11.

The Bible refers to "God's spoken word" as the *water for our faith*. Every born-again believer has been given "the measure of faith."

> *For by the grace given to me I say to everyone among you not to think of himself more highly than he ought to think, but to think with sober judgment, each according to the measure of faith that God has assigned.*
>
> —Romans 12:3

When we begin to speak God's word and promises over and above our circumstances, our faith begins to grow stronger and stronger because that is the intended purpose of his words. They are faith-filled words sent to water our faith, keeping it alive and strong in our spirit.

They are both spiritual forces; when once connected, powerful inconceivable things begin to happen in your body as well in your life. It will be hard for the human mind to conceive this spiritual truth at first, but the more of God's words we hear and speak, it becomes part of us, and by this process, our mind will begin to line up, believing in the unseen more than the seen.

Do not conform any longer to the pattern of this world, but be transformed by the renewing of your mind. Then you will be able to test and approve what God's will is—his good, pleasing and perfect will.
—Romans 12:2

Some of us have heard or said at one point, "That person lies so much, he believes his own lies." This is very true, and faith works the same way. We confess it until it becomes a part of us; only it's not a lie, it's God's spoken promises regarding our life, and since he is bound by the integrity of his words, he honors every spoken word of his. Our spirit will always hold firm to the truth because it is a part of God.

> *As the rain and snow come down from heaven and do not return to it without watering the earth and making it bud and flourish, so that it yield seed for the sower and bread for the eater, <u>so is in my word that goes out from my mouth: it will not return to me empty, but will accomplish what I desire and achieve the purpose for which I sent it.</u> Then you will go out in joy and be led forth into peace.*
>
> —Isaiah 55:10-12

But in order to live in this peace, you have to do your part by applying the basic principles. We do this by first repenting of our sins and turning to God in need of a savior, and in him we become one with the divine infinite nature of God. We must then believe what the Christ, the anointed man of God, has said regarding "faith, power, and the kingdom of God within us."

Again, out of ignorance we believe those things to be true for Christ alone and only for that period of time when in fact these things have been acknowledged from the beginning of time. Christ was sent to demonstrate the administration of our divine nature through the power of faith in the spirit of God.

After his crucifixion, all his disciples demonstrated his power along with countless others. During the centuries to follow, Christian spiritual leaders were also well advanced in their faith with power to heal the sick, and they preached the gospel of Christ and the ministry of the Holy Spirit as Jesus instructed.

This ministry exists today and is being demonstrated all over the world. But just as Jesus has experienced during his healing ministry, these teachings are being rejected, calling it blasphemy mainly because of the conviction one feels when faced with the revelation and knowledge of truth. This convicting truth places some of our mistakes, diseases, shortcomings, and the destruction of our children back into the hands of its rightful owner, ourselves. This is in fact a hard pill to swallow but nevertheless the truth.

Jesus explains the working of the Holy Spirit:

> *When he comes he will convict the world of guilt in regard to sin and righteousness.*
>
> —John 16:8

Jesus said . . . go into the entire world and preach the good news to all creation. Whoever believes and is baptized will be saved but whoever does not believe will be condemned. And these signs will accompany those who believe: in my name they will drive out demons; they will speak in new tongues; they will pick up snakes with their hands and when they drink deadly poison, it will not hurt them, they will place their hands on the sick and they will get well.

—Mark 16:15-18

Christ was speaking in regard to total protection in the blessing.

To deny these teachings to be true for you is to reject the grace of God and whom he created you to be. We all heard the phrase *"God is everywhere and he sees everything."* Most of us like to believe God dwells only in the heavenly realms and is watching us from above when in fact he is omnipresent, which means his life-giving spirit is everywhere and in everybody.

We know this is true because his presence is demonstrated from the power of the sun to the very depths of this earth, through every natural force in nature, which shapes and recreates the earth. His presence governs the fowl in the air to the fish of the sea. We too demonstrate his presence within us through the power of his spirit, which presides over all things in our earthly kingdom. By accepting these spiritual conditions as a possibility for you, your mind would then become receptive to further possibilities of this power we carry within ourselves, and it is through the measure of your faith that will be the determining factor of his word operating in your life.

If we can begin to stay faithful in speaking his word above our circumstances until it becomes real to us, then God will be faithful to honor it. When and how it will happen should be of no concern to you. We are and will always be limited in our thinking when compared to the mind of God who formed a perfect system for our existence.

Against all hope, Abraham in hope believed and so became the father of many nations, just as it had been said to him, "So shall your offspring be." Without weakening in his faith, he faced the fact that his body was as good as dead—since he was about a hundred years old—and that Sarah's womb was also dead. Yet he did not waver through unbelief regarding the promise of God, but was strengthened in his faith and gave glory to God, being fully persuaded that God had power to do what he had promised. This is why "it was credited to him as righteousness." The words "it was credited to him" were written not for him alone, but also for us, to whom God will credit righteousness—for us who believe in him who raised Jesus our Lord from the dead.

—Romans 4:18-24

Chapter 6

Light on Faith

The Root of Faith

Faith is being sure of what we hope for and certain of what we do not see. By faith we understand that the universe was formed at God's command, so that what is seen was not made out of the visible.

—Hebrews 11:1-3

We were all given a measure of faith but many of us were never taught the purpose of faith or how to use it so we have lived our lives putting our faith in things that are seen, which does not promote faith but fear.

Faith is the beginning the spiritual component of all things that currently exist and is accompanied by power. When faith is applied to healing, supernatural health is summoned. When faith is applied to wealth, supernatural financial provisions are provided. In the same way, when fear is applied to affliction, those conditions become your own. Fear is the flip side of faith, but faith and fear are governed by the same spiritual law because they are both based on your belief system and are accompanied by strong emotions. Because they are a parallel power that stand opposed one to the other, one cancels out the other. It's just a matter of what you perceive as truth that will be the determining factor of what you have conditions you have called to yourself. There is no middle ground, we're either living one way or the other. How we respond to our current circumstances will be the measuring stick for our faith or our fear.

In order to operate in faith, it's imperative to think of things that are desired especially in times of adversity, speaking the promises of God on them (I can, I will, I am, I have). As the mental picture is formed in your spiritual mind its imperative to hold that vision through all adversity because that vision is the seed that's needed to plant the new crop in which you are hoping for. The more you hold it, the more real it becomes and by this process you are increasing your faith in the things you desire which will cause you to believe as if it's already a reality in your life, believing that those things desired will follow the demand through faith. That's being sure of what we hope for and certain of what we do not see. That's what faith is, that's what it does, and that's how it works.

To consciously live by faith is to believe in the end result before it becomes a physical reality, putting all your faith in what God has already accomplished through Christ, believing what he said about faith and not waiting for an answer, but knowing the answer before it shows up. Any form of success or victory is based on this process. The same thing is true for those who act upon something for the good, almost convinced that it will fail but succeeded nonetheless. The fact that they acted on it proves some measure of faith in it, or they wouldn't have acted. So their mustard-seed faith brought victory.

> *I tell you the truth, if you have faith as small as a mustard seed, you can say to this mountain, "Move from here to there" and it will move. Nothing will be impossible for you.*
> —Matthew 17:20

In light of this verse, we all know that the mountain Christ speaks about is not a literal mountain, but the thing that is blocking our way of success in any are. We live out our faith every day whether it be faith in the good or the bad; either one correlates with its object in the natural world and produces conditions in accordance to the nature of the faith or fear implied.

This truth is so foreign compared to old church laws and its teaching that it may be hard for one to grasp the true concept of it, yet it is more real and has more life than our own existence. We were taught to fear God and his wrath as opposed to honoring him through our faith based his goodness in order to receive the life he has designed for us through faith.

And without faith it is impossible to please God, because anyone who comes to him must believe that he exists and that he rewards those who earnestly seek him.
—Hebrews 11:6

The holy ministry of Christ was based on faith and acts done in faith. He told all those who followed him to *"go out into all the world and preach the gospel of good news and peace."*

It's time that we all acknowledge that there is a world within us that responds by faith to the things of God that allows us to receive all that he has already given us by his grace.

Fear, on the other hand, works in the same way. You think of the worst thing that can happen to you. You speak the promises of Satan (I'm going to die from this, it's hereditary, I was bound to get it, nothing never goes right for me). Then you act it out by doing nothing to oppose it, accepting those things as they come to you as if it's already a reality in your life simply by preparing for the worst, and faith in that fear will cause those things to become true *for you*.

Take a moment to think about it; you have what you believed you could have, nothing more and nothing less. If this were not true then you wouldn't have acted with the intention of having. What you don't have already, believing that it's possible for you, will, by spiritual law, come to you; good or bad, it's just a matter of *time*. The Bible says that there will be *seedtime and harvest* as long as the earth endures. The law of return guarantees it. Your thinking, your words, and the things you act on or respond to according to the gospel of Christ are the seeds for the conditions of which you will live, and the lives of your children will be harvested under those same conditions. This is a very simple truth but, for most, a very difficult concept to comprehend because it places the blame back on us. But the truth seeker will begin to consider the possibility of wrong thinking as being the cause of many of his afflictions by simply paying close attention to his thought life and examining its content, looking intently at his own character, ego, and pride like a lion on a prowl for any evidence of life.

Consciously having faith in the things we don't see could be a challenge to most people; after all, we've been living by our physical senses all of our life. But let the truth be told, we've been living by faith subconsciously all along, creating the very life before us in advance. We have been told not to judge a book by its cover, see what's inside, and there you will find the truth. However, the reality is, we have been living by and judging everything by its cover. What we could see, feel, taste, hear, and smell is more real to us than the spiritual administration of this world. But to live by faith is to believe in the unseen element of a thing, not in the physical things we can already see and feel because those are all manifested effects. They have reached their highest potential of growth, coming from the unseen realm of life into clear view, and can now only serve its purpose for the time that it has left to exist. It becomes worldly and anything that comes into this world has limited value. We have to look past the obvious and start at the beginning of that thing. So then you begin to ask yourself hypothetically, "Where did this TV come from? What is the beginning of it?" It started with a thought, and thoughts are spiritual. A television is the harvest of the seed, a creative idea, planted in that person's mind. The creator of that television was sure of what he hoped for and was certain of what he did not see. The evidence of that television was already a spiritual fact in the person's mind before he brought it into physical manifestation. And when that object ceases to exist in the physical realm of life, the blueprint still remains in the mind of its creator and becomes a gift to many as we adopt this creative idea, adding our own creative personality to it.

The ministry of Jesus teaches us that the kingdom of God functions like a garden within every man, woman, or child. It only knows to grow what has been put in it, in which those seeds are responsible for our dreams and disasters. This is an indication that the harvest simply depends on the farmer. That makes us the farmer of our lives and our children's life since we're responsible for their growth and well-being. If the roots of a tree die, so does the branches and the vines; therefore, the root is responsible for what it produces.

> *Make a tree good and its fruit will be good, or make a tree bad and its fruit will be bad, for a tree is recognized by its fruit. You brood of vipers, how can you who are evil say anything good? For out of the overflow of the heart the mouth speaks. The good man brings good things out of the good stored up in him, and the evil man brings evil things out of the evil stored up in him.*
>
> —Matthew 12: 33-35

Just as flowers grow from a seed planted in a natural garden and grows up to become physical material, so do your beliefs, words, acts, and deeds in the spirit. Everything on this earth was manifested from a thought, not one thing came by the physical material that was brought forth. Sure, we can now manufacture duplicate material to create more of the same product, but the beginning of that product dwells in the unseen spiritual realm of someone's mind. Though the product is a fact, the truth remains with its source, faith, love, and imagination.

It is our duty to gather a clear understanding of how life works through the spiritual realm of life, only then will we be able to navigate our lives into the direction it was predestined to go. When we live by the spirit, the spirit of love, we allow the power of God to work through us bringing us to our highest and greatest good.

Once we can begin to understand that all things in life were formed first by the spiritual mind, only then will we gain the power to consciously create a life desirable, one worth living by faith and as a direct result, our children will also bear good fruit.

According to His Will

I would like to make something very clear before continuing on to my final chapter in regards to faith. Many bible teachers and pastors have taken faith to the extreme by leading many to believe that whatever they ask in faith they may receive. This kind of thinking is false doctrine. We can only receive what God has already provided through his covenant. We can only be blessed through the blessings that are within his covenant. For example, in regard to marriage, you may pray for a husband or a wife because the blessing of marriage is within the covenant. But you cannot pray for another man's wife or another woman's husband, nor will you be blessed in doing so, because adultery is not in his covenant therefore, it is not in accordance with will. In fact, anyone living in adultery is living under a curse and will live a life of total destruction according to these scripture: (Proverbs 5: 1-23, Proverbs 6:20-35, Proverbs 7:1-36, Matthew 5:27-28, Matthew 5:32, Matthew 15:19, Hosea 3:1, John 8:4, Deuteronomy 5:18, and so on).

One can pray for financial provision because it's within his will that we are all provided for, but the motives have to be for the good of the whole, free of any selfish indulgences. According to James 4:2-3,

> *You want something but don't get it. You kill and covet, but you cannot have what you want. You quarrel and fight. You do not have, because you do not ask God. When you ask, you do not receive, because you ask with wrong motives, that you may spend what you get on your pleasures.*
>
> —James 4:2-3

In other words, if you have a million dollar need for the common good of his kingdom, whether it be to spread his word, or to begin some charitable organization that will restore lives honor of his love and grace, then God had a million dollar answer for you. But if the motive behind your asking is first for you and yours with the intent to give once you have become established, then the answer is no and anything you have gained through wrong motives, you will loose as as a result, it will be as if you've never had.

We can pray that God forgives those who have sinned against us or caused us harm. But he will not honor a prayer rooted in strife, revenge, anger, bitterness, or unforgiveness.

For if you forgive men when they sin against you, your heavenly father will also forgive you. But if you do not forgive men their sins, your father will not forgive you.

—Matthew 6:15

Therefore, as God's chosen people, holy and dearly loved, clothe yourself with humility, gentleness and patience. Bear with each other and forgive whatever grievances you may have against one another. Forgive as the Lord forgave you. And of all these virtues, put on love which binds them together in perfect unity.

—Colossians 3:12-14

So do not throw away your confidence; it will be richly rewarded. You need to persevere so that when you have done the will of God, you will receive what he has promised. For in just a very little while, "He who is coming will come and will not delay. But my righteous one will live by faith. And if he shrinks back, I will not be pleased with him." But we are not of those who shrink back and are destroyed, but of those who believe and are saved.

—Hebrews 10:39-35

Borrowed Faith v. Grounded Faith

Far too often do we accept a theory or a concept to be true based on someone else's word. We often swear by the word of some reliable person, never putting in the time or effort to find the source behind their word. In most cases, if it sounds good and reasonable, we accept it as truth. The problem with that is there is no true understanding behind the concept given, and if we have not developed a complete understanding of how something can happen or be, we then limit that thing from becoming a reality in our own lives because there's no real faith behind it. But so long as faith is applied to something, it will forever work for us. Whether it's there to stay depends on its source.

Those who have faith in themselves are more than likely to accomplish and overcome anything they put their mind to than those who don't simply because these people believe that the vision that's on the inside of them is bigger than their circumstances. Those who have accomplished their goal; once being oblivious of the hand of God working in their lives have later come to realize that although they took all the credit for being talented due to the hard labor of which they themselves invested, they realize in the end that they were given a divine gift that was far bigger than themselves simply because their reward turned out to be much greater than they could've ever envisioned. Those who use their gift for the benefit of the common good towards humanity, to the glory of God know under no uncertain terms that their gift was given to them, developed, and pruned for the very position in which they now stand. And although others have chosen to exploit their gift to promote sexual immorality, violence or greed to the destruction of others, the fact that they believed that they can turn rags into riches afforded them the opportunity to transcend. But in either case, once accomplished, they recollect in awe on all the abundant opportunities that became available by no effort of their own, that all the events and opportunities were governed by a hand much bigger than their own.

There are many people in this world who are unaware of their divine purpose or gift. This does not mean that God has not given them a gift of their own. In most cases, people become so blinded by the troubles of this world, that they become enslaved to its conditions therefore, they are unable to develop it. The system of this fallen world becomes their source. Then there are those who have inherited wealth and finds no need to make proper use of their gift due to their financial freedom to self indulge. These people are blinded by their greed. Still there are others whom from the start, through desire, find themselves wanting something more out of life from an early age and so their gift is realized at the birth of aspiration. Still yet there are those who have been through hell and back only to realize that the only way to fly is straight and so they aspire to higher ground in search of a resting place, ultimately serving no real purpose. These people are held captive in their false state of contentment due to their lack of aspiration.

Living in this world in light of all its troubles can lead one to believe that God gives special gifts to some and not to others, but that is not the truth. He gives to us all. What separates us all and puts us in this class or that class are three things; Faith, vision, and aspiration, because those three things are the catalyst to all created things.

> *Delight yourself in the Lord and he will give you the desires of your heart.*
>
> —Psalms 37: 4

When we delight ourselves in the Lord, we begin to live according to his will. He places his desires on the inside of us, and as a result, they become our desires. God leads and guides us according to his plan, purpose, and glory so that we can live a life of power and influence.

The truth is, he wants us to step out on faith and pursue the good things he has placed in our hearts, because if he placed them there, then there is a reason for it. He doesn't do anything without a plan. His divine gifts are appointed before birth and are brought to life through aspiration and faith. As children, they acted on it by pretending and imagining themselves in that place. As they got older, they sought after it with diligence and zeal. Silent prayers were consistent in their heart. As I said in the previous chapters, anything meditated on for any length of time is seed sown and a form of prayer. As the dream ripened, it became a reality in their heart. They put no limitations on what they could achieve by envisioning success; therefore, by faith, love, and desire, their dreams became realities. They simply asked, believed, and received. They were able to receive all that God had in store for them by simply believing that it was theirs for the taking, that their circumstances did not define who they were and what they could achieve. They stepped out on something that was far bigger than themselves.

> *And without faith it is impossible to please him, for whoever would draw near to God must believe that he exists and that he rewards those who seek him.*
> —Hebrews 11:6

Our faith is the catalyst to all things obtained good and bad. Whether you believe you can or can't will become true for you and your life will be the revealed of that truth. As a tree is known by it's fruit, every thing hidden will be revealed. It's just a matter of time.

To have grounded faith means to have have faith in God, believing he created you with the ability to accomplish your highest and greatest good therefore, you have the ability on the inside of you to overcome any difficulty or succeed at anything and in that faith, he will sustain you.

I have a saying: if there is a passion or a dream on the inside of you that is bigger than what you can achieve in your own strength, it is from God. Because this dream requires faith proves that it was placed there from God because we're in need of his faith in order to achieve it. So if we step out on faith, he guides us through it. Therefore, the promise is the reward of our faith.

On the other hand, the dreams and desires that are planned and created by us only require practical applications in order to see that thing through and the benefit your actions provided, will only have a temporary value. This should be the measuring stick that will determine whose path you're on.

God is a big god who does big things so that not one of us can boast about what *we* have done but what *he* has accomplished through us. If a person is presumed qualified by the world based on his educational status, then we will justify his reward based on his hard work rather than the work of God operating in his life through faith. For this reason, he will in many cases, use the least educated, the one who's considered through the eyes of the world, less likely too succeed to accomplish his will, so that his power is revealed. This is to keep us in remembrance of him and to show the world his great works so that they too might believe and receive all he has given us by grace through faith.

So that in the coming ages he might show the immeasurable riches of his grace in kindness toward us in Christ Jesus. For by grace you have been saved through faith. And this is not your own doing; it is the gift of God, not a result of works, so that no one may boast. For we are his workmanship created in Christ Jesus for good works, which God prepared in advance for us to do.

—Ephesians 7:10

Grounded Faith

Let's examine the lives some of the most successful superstars we know of today. Some performed since childhood, whether it was in the privacy of their home or on stage. It came natural to them, and they did it effortlessly with confidence and desire. They had an obvious passion and pretended they were already stars from the start of the thought. The leadership position they held in their group, be it in childhood or in the later stages of life, became their position in their success.

It's obvious that the lead singers acquired the most success in comparison to the rest of the group and became even bigger stars on their own, all becoming legendary. These people had faith, vision, and passion for success and power. They dreamt it day and night and saw themselves doing it. Desire along with faith and silent prayer (vision) brought it to them. If they can recognize through whom that power came, they can never lose it because they placed that power with God and located it within themselves. They have what I call *grounded faith*.

Borrowed Faith

Now let's take look at the rest of the group. They put their fate in the hands of the lead singer. Their inferiority is obvious based on their position in the group, which clearly declares, "I'll get in where I can fit in." They rely on the lead singer to get them to fame, and fame they shall get, but the power remains with its source. Once the lead decides to take on new challenges on their own, they take the power with them, leaving the others to fend for themselves either in shame or disappointment. In most cases, you never hear from the rest of the group again. They are left behind, never achieving their full measure of success. This is what I like to call *borrowed faith*.

It worked for a time but left with its source. In doing so, their minds went back to its original way of thinking, thoughts of limitations and lack, and because they placed their faith in the unit as a whole, when a part left, the unit fell apart. The vision died. This is the result of a crop failure. Seeds were not sown on solid ground.

The synopsis of these two scenarios is the star found the source of power from within, and the others didn't. The star had faith in him or herself while the others had faith in the group. The star desired power, the others desired fame. Power brings forth success, honor, and an abundant life; fame brings forth opportunity. The others believed they *could be* a star. The star *was always* a star.

A great spiritual leader and teacher once said, "You cannot draw from the highest power if you depend always on the help of others, if so you are absorbing their faith, which will work only for a time. When that of which you borrow is cut off, your spirits will go back to the domain of material belief. You have never learned to increase your faith through the silent demand of the supreme power. You had never really drawn from the right source."

If you noticed, most celebrities, if they never did before, give glory to God for all their achievements. They know within their spirit under no uncertain terms that something bigger than themselves brought them there because what they imagined they could be was far less than what was ultimately in store for them. They become astonished at the power within and praise him for being the source of it all.

I encourage you to observe an example in the book of Matthew 14:27-31. Jesus was observed walking on water by his disciples and they became terrified claiming it to be a ghost of some sort. Jesus said to them,

> "Take courage, it is I, don't be afraid." Peter replied, "If it is you, tell me to come to you on the water and I will come." Jesus said, "Come." Peter got down out of the boat and walked on the water toward Jesus. But when he saw the wind, he was afraid and began to sink and cried out for Jesus to save him. As Jesus did so, he said <u>"You of little faith, why did you doubt?"</u>

Christ demonstrated the power of faith. He implied that Peter's faith failed due to his unbelief. And had he not doubted himself, he would have walked on water by his own power. So Peter was able to walk for only a short time as long as his eyes were focused Christ. But since Christ was made to be like us (human) yet equipped with divine powers, he was a living example of who we are in him and how we are to respond to unexpected circumstances.

But before Jesus confirmed that it was him, he demanded that Peter "take courage," suggesting to Peter that courage is an unseen spiritual force that conquers all challenges in life. This was an example of borrowed faith. Who's going to save you when I'm gone?

Jesus said on many occasions, "Have faith, your faith has healed you, ye of little faith." Although he demonstrated his power throughout his ministry, many were unable to receive the gift of grace due to their unbelief.

Chapter 7

The Law of Return

In the previous chapters, I have revealed to you the power of God and the administration of his kingdom. I have shown you through scriptural teaching that his kingdom is governed by seedtime and harvest laws, which are spiritual laws that govern the operations of this present world. Our human spirit is known as the ground, and our words are known as the seed to be planted. Every seed will produce a crop of its kind in due season. It's the law of natural and spiritual farming in which all life-forms operate. This operation is governed by the law of return. Each seed planted, be it in man or in the earth, produces a harvest of its kind, some thirty, some sixty, some one hundred fold, the Bible says.

Let's use a farmer as an example. A farmer plants orange seeds into the ground and produces a harvest of oranges. Each orange returns to him a hundredfold based on the amount of seeds within each orange. He now has a harvest of oranges to sell that will bring him a financial harvest along with more seeds to plant at no cost to him. This man understands the laws of seedtime and harvest by making use of his return.

> *Give and it will be given to you. A good measure, pressed down, shaken together and running over, will be poured into your lap. For with the measure you use, it will be measured to you.*

Everything in life has a return of more than what was given, for the good or bad, whether it's time, energy, money, words, or deeds. With every action, there's a reaction. With every cause, there's an effect. This is the *gospel* in which Jesus *preached*. This is the good news he preached to the poor, sick, and afflicted. This is the reason the Bible teaches us to "pay close attention to his words and not to let them out of our sight"; words have the power to bring into existence life or death.

> *Likewise the tongue is a small part of the body, but it makes great boasts. Consider what a great forest is set on fire by a small spark. The tongue also is a fire, a world of evil amongst the parts of the body. It corrupts the whole person, sets the whole course of his life on fire, and it is set on fire by hell.*
>
> —James 3:5-6

Jesus explains in Mark 4:13-20 the secret kingdom of God.

The secret kingdom of God has been given to you. The farmer sows the word. Some people are like seed along the path where the word is sown. As soon as they hear it, Satan comes and takes away the word that was sown in them.

Satan will try to convince us that the word of God cannot change our circumstances by bringing forth an obstacle by way of your physical senses, causing you to revert back to your normal way of thinking.

Others hear the word and receive it with joy. But since they have no root [no faith], they last only a short time.

The gospel of Jesus is good news to you. To understand that you have been given victory in Christ Jesus and power to overcome Satan is music to your ears and makes sense to you, but you have no wisdom or spiritual understanding of how that can be true for you and as a result, your lack of faith fails you.

Still others like seed hear the word, but worries of this life, the deceitfulness of wealth and the desire for other things come in and choke the word making it unfruitful.

This parable illustrates a persons mental attitude toward life and wealth in addition to wrong motives. These people are spiritually discerned. They deal with life from a physical standpoint alone and are governed by their failing circumstances. They do not understand that money is not a master but a servant. They hunger for the riches of this world to satisfy their beastly appetite instead of the true riches of God which are wisdom, power, faith, and love, and by this, they are unable to sustain what they have gained.

Yet others hear the word, accept it, and produce a crop, thirty, sixty or even a hundred times what was sown.

These people accept the word and its provisions. They have gained insight into God's secret administration as he revealed it to them through his word. They increased their faith by studying, meditation and confession. They accepted

God's promises for their lives and realized that they are heirs with Christ. They became fully persuaded of their position of power and authority in this earth and over Satan. They have wisdom in regards to spiritual farming. They resist the temptation to fall away in spite of what has been presented to them by thinking and speaking in accordance to the nature of the desired harvest, fully aware of the power behind their words.

He goes on to teach in Mark 4:22,

Whatever is hidden or sown in your heart is meant to be brought out in the open.

Again, Jesus is explaining the secret to God's kingdom. "Everyone must reap what you sow."

Anything taking form in this world was created from the unseen, from someone's thoughts, started as a seed.

Just as an apple seed takes root in the unseen, becoming a physical thing; babies are created from the unseen, becoming a physical being. Our words being created from the unseen taking form. We may never know in the physical realm how elements are drawn to its source to create such life on earth.

But we can be sure that God is the ultimate farmer of earth and man because we were made perfect.

> *A man scatters seed on the ground. Night and day, whether he sleeps or gets up, the seed sprouts and grows, though he does not know how. All by itself, it produces grain, first the stalk, then the head, then the full kernel in the head. As soon as the grain is ripe, he puts a sickle to it, because the harvest has come.*
>
> —Mark 4:26

All material things we possess originated from someone's thoughts. And you planted it in your heart *(your spirit),* with words, before you held it in your hand. God is the biggest and greatest eternal living spirit who created this world from his thoughts by speaking words.

> *By faith we understand that the universe was formed at God's command, so that what is seen was not made out of what was visible.*
>
> —Hebrews 11:3

He is the supreme example of spiritual farming. The kingdom of God is for those who believe. And those who believe can operate from the kingdom God has placed within us. This is God's will for your life.

The parable of the mustard seed says; the best parable used to describe the kingdom of God is like a mustard seed, the smallest seed you can plant. But when the plant grows, it becomes the largest plant in the garden, with such big branches that even the birds of the air can take shade.

—Mark 4:30

Chapter 8

The Tree of Life

When we can begin using our full thinking potential by planting our desires firmly through faith, only then will we begin to understand the administration of God's secret kingdom that lies within every man, woman, and child.

Christ refers to our life here on earth as that of a tree. In John 15:1, he says that he is the vine and we are the branches, but the father is the gardener who prunes and cuts off the branches that do not bear fruit. But he makes clear that a tree will be known by its fruit. With Christ being the vine, residing at the center of our lives, those who are in him have a sure foundation to build on; therefore, we will most certainly produce good things.

So let a standing tree inspire us to live by faith. I believe it was put there as a physical example of our life. Just look at it. At a glance, you see nothing but a stalk with some leaves. You think nothing of its purpose or beauty. Well, let's take a closer look.

The seed of a tree was created to perfection by God, the source of all things. When the seed is planted, the seed itself dies, and the substance within that seed governed by the law of growth, by the very nature of it, produces grain for its new form and growth. In the unseen elements of the earth, the roots migrate down into the earth becoming one with its source. It then spirals upward, eager to express itself into physical form. Once manifested into form, it utilizes its resources already provided in advance for its vitality by absorbing the oxygen, energy, and light which is the substance needed for every living thing on earth that only God has the ability to provide. As it begins to bear fruit, the birds flock to its branches, making it their home, relying on it for protection and food. It provides shade, comfort, oxygen, food, strength, and most of all peace to all living things on earth, and we are not excluded for we are also drawn to it. We also rely and benefit from all of its resources.

But then there comes a season of testing where its strength will be tested against the forces of nature. For a time like job, it will be stripped of all its material possessions and become barren. When this process takes place, every living thing will flee from its presence and abandon it. Although it looks like death, it is a purifying process needed for its growth and stability. As it forms a tough outer layer, it takes courage against all adversity, staying true to its purpose of strength, beauty, life, and abundance in spite of its current circumstances. Its future harvest is dependent upon its ability to withstand the storm.

> *Consider it pure joy, my brothers, whenever you face trials of many kinds, because you know that the testing of your faith develops perseverance. Perseverance must finish its work so that you may be mature and complete, not lacking anything.*
> —James 1:2-4

In truth, a tree is a direct reflection of the very life we live from the seed to the fruit. But we were created for a much higher purpose. God has created so many other examples of life with purpose for us to learn from. We live on this earth in harmony with other life forces, not realizing that we are one with them, sharing, needing, and absorbing the same elements from the same source. We live as trees live. What separates us and make us more valuable to God is that we were made in his image and likeness with his spirit and power to create as he is our creator.

Paul, the apostle, prayed, "I pray that out of his glorious riches, he may strengthen you with power through his spirit in your inner being, so that Christ may dwell in your heart through faith."

We are one with the infinite power, a thinking, living, speaking spirit as God is, being made greater than all physical things with powers to create a life desirable through *faith*.

Every living thing God has created, every animal, fish, bird, mammal all live by instinct, without the spirit of God and is given in full measure all that is needed for its function here on earth.

Mountains, deserts, caves, forests, and even rivers are governed by the spirit of its nature, recreating itself through a spiritual source provided by God, and these things exist in abundance.

But we were given the creative ability to think and to live by creative thought. We live by the choices we make every minute of every day, and the Lord in his mercy, love, and grace has made us the pilot of our life's direction. We get to choose who we serve, how we want to live, and what we are to become. We can either submit our lives to the Spirit of God by trusting him to lead and guide us safely through the storms of life or we can choose to take our chances against life's turbulence in our own strength separating ourselves from his grace. Now I'm not implying that we have Power over God. His will, will ultimately prevail in spite of the choices we make however, our level of comfort during our journey is compromised in our decision to go our own way.

This day I call heaven and earth as witnesses against you that I have set before you life and death, blessings and curses. <u>Now choose life</u>, so that you and your children may live. And that you may love the Lord your God, listen to his voice, and hold fast to him.
—Deuteronomy 30:19-20

Now fear the Lord and serve him with all faithfulness. Throw away the gods your forefathers worshiped beyond the River and in Egypt, and serve the Lord. <u>But if serving the Lord seems undesirable to you, then choose for yourselves this day whom you will serve.</u>
—Joshua 24:15

This *will* lies within our consciousness. The conscious is that presence in the center of our mind, behind our eyes, looking out. It's not our eyeballs that see. Eyes are merely a tool in which the soul uses to see physical objects in order to keep us from harming ourselves. But they're not a necessity. When the eyes are incapable of seeing the light of day, the mind turns its focus inward to its thoughts and imagination. We know it as the third eye, the eye that can see what our physical eyes cannot. The spiritual eye lives by faith. With this insight, we are no longer moved by what we see or feel, we are only moved by what we believe and all of our judgments based on the truth we hold in our mind and so our life will reveal that truth.

All of our hopes and dreams can become a possibility if we can learn to look to our inner vision as truth, and because the world cannot see it, they cannot oppose it. As a tree expresses itself from the seed that's been planted into the earth, the same thing is true in regards to our soul. It's fed through what we entertain in our minds and because the human spirit is life in itself, it works with the soul, therefore it gives life to the things we believe. It produces a crop in accordance to the nature of the thought given to it. Everything grows into a form of expression. Stevie Wonder, Stephen Hawking, Albert Einstein, Galileo, along with many others all turned their focus within and accomplished what most of us wouldn't dare to attempt given the best circumstances.

If we live according to our supernatural nature, our spiritual mind, we will begin to understand the love God has created us with and that he has created us more valuable to him than we think. If an abundant supply of everything we could ever need and want is everywhere in this earth, then it belongs to us; it was meant to be in our lives not just before our eyes. What father would tease his children with good things? He has made a provision for all things obtainable through the knowledge of whom he is and who he created us to be.

God has given us the earth to express his creative nature in it with spiritual and natural laws that govern it through the power of his spirit. He has given us a never-ending supply of all that is needed to live on this earth and enjoy it. The laws of science will always tempt us into fear of lack. It teaches that the sun will eventually lose it's energy, that we are running out of water and all the natural resources that God has provided to sustain us. This is because, they look at the word from a human point of view, deeming us to be the source life.

But the truth is; God has provided us with everything that we need to sustain ourselves on earth until his second coming. There was never a shortage of water because it's a substance that we are unable to produce in the measure for which it's needed and same thing is true in regards to the sun.

His promises are plain and sufficient enough for us. The sun rises every morning for us; the moon is a promise for the night sky. Water is the key element to life and is abundant and available to all living things. As we wake with morning consciousness, that's God's promise for another opportunity to be creative and make a difference in our lives and in the lives of others. And with our life, we get to create our desires through the power of faith in the thing that's desired.

All that we would ever need for our survival is generously supplied no matter what circumstances we currently live in even in spite of our wickedness. The sun shines on the wicked and the righteous. There"s no favoritism involved when it comes to the things of God. All that we need to live is here; we only have to believe that it is ours for the taking to receive it.

And God is able to make all grace abound to you, so that in all things at all times; having all that you need, you will abound in every good work.
—2 Corinthians 9:8

Chapter 9

Health: The Law of Life

Praise the Lord, O my soul, and forget not his benefits- who forgives all your sins and heals all your diseases, who redeems your life from the pit and crowns you with love and compassion, who satisfies your desires with good things so that your youth is renewed like an eagle.

—Psalms 103:-5

There is a spiritual law of life in which all living things are created. This law operates in the principle of love and it's fruit are perfect health, strength, and vigor, which is the perfection of life. This law of life is the very reason we grow, reproduce, and strive to achieve the best life has to offer. It causes us to express ourselves, and because of this, we excel toward higher living. It is the cause behind every moment of life and the life surrounding us.

Behind every spiritual law there's a principal by which that law operates. The principal the governs the law of life is health. When the principal of health is in positive motion, it causes a transformation in the human system by casting off old elements of decay and returning it to new life. This is a spiritual process from which all life is renewed. Animals shed their fur, birds cast off their feathers, and trees cast off its leaves in order to bring forth new life. But our transformation process is different than that of any other living thing. We live by our thoughts therefore, our casting off shows up in the form of sickness.

Since we live by our thoughts, we are constantly creating our life in advance. But the intended purpose of the human spirit is to bring forth and maintain life in our bodies by the power of right thought expressed through words. This is the source of perfect health.

> *The spirit gives life; the flesh counts for nothing. The words I have spoken to you are spirit and they are life.*
>
> —John 6:6

Our human body is nothing more than a physical expression of our human spirit, and our spirit desires to live according to its full potential, bringing forth the most perfect life in the body given to it; however, if a person is oblivious to the laws of life, they have limited the human spirits ability to perform at it's peak in accordance with truth by feeding it an enormous amount of error or false beliefs by just simply thinking the wrong thoughts, speaking the wrong words, and by eating the wrong foods. So in order to put this principle of health into action, we must think and speak according to its nature.

> *Listen closely to my words. Do not let them out of your sight; keep them within your heart, for they are life to those who find them and health to a man's whole body.*
>
> —Proverbs 4:20-22

During my lifetime, I have learned how unhealthy habits and genetic diseases will affect my body; however, I was never taught about the magnificence of the human spirit and its life-giving purpose. Nor was I told of the body's ability to respond to our thoughts, that it lives our thoughts; therefore, our bodies are indeed a product of our mind. Because we lack proper knowledge of the basic principles of life, when damage and decay show up, we have no faith in the human system and its ability to restore itself. By this we agree with the body's current state of decay which is certain to assist us in the destruction we hold in our mind. Where the mind goes, the body is sure to follow.

Just as thoughts are the spiritual substance for all created things that physically exist, the same thing is true where our health is concerned. Our minds feed our human spirit. Our spirit being made in the likeness of God is no respecter of words; it only knows to grow what's been planted in it, be it good or ill will.

> *The good man brings good things out of the good stored up in his heart, and the evil man brings evil things out of the evil stored up in his heart. For out of the overflow of his heart his mouth speaks.*
>
> —Luke 6:45

> *Make a tree good and its fruit will be good, or make a tree bad and its fruit will be bad, for a tree is recognized by its fruit. You brood of vipers, how can you who are evil say anything good? For out of the overflow of the heart the mouth speaks.*
>
> —Matthew 12:33-35

We will most certainly reap what we sow in every arena of life. The law of return is always in motion, and we live by it every second of the day. We are always setting up our future circumstances in advance, our health is not excluded. Therefore, whatever is established in our physical bodies today is a by-product or an expression of what we thought yesterday, last week, last month, or even a year ago. Time is measured in accordance to our faith; the stronger the faith in whatever we believe to be true for us, the quicker the results. The thoughts that will reach its full expression are the thoughts that are most established in our spirit, the things we most believe about ourselves. We are taken by surprise in our hardships out of ignorance in regard to the spiritual principles of life.

Poor health doesn't just show up; nothing is ever created at a moment's notice. That's an illusion that has been impressed in our minds manufactured by Satan to get us off track so that we would respond to our difficulty with shock and fear. All this is done in hopes to cancel out our faith, to lose ground in the things of God in order to create an inroad for more schemes and manipulations that is sure to make our lives pure hell if we choose to believe in them.

We now understand that faith and fear both have corresponding power, but it is not so much a matter of power but of compensation. They both operate in the law of return and will return to you in physical form, your own thoughts.

I am not implying that Satan has power to control our lives; on the contrary, we give him that power by responding to his evil influences by way of fear, frustration, anger, strife, worry, or by any other negative response that we ourselves apply to any given situation. Just as faith is a positive response to what God has already done, fear is also a positive response to what Satan presents as truth.

We must think perfect love, perfect health, and long life if we ever hope to have it. When we begin to train our minds to focus on the good in life, the things we most desire will be a challenge for many at first. In fact, it may be the hardest thing you have ever decided to carry out, even worse than physical labor for most. This is because when people live in error for so long, it is hard to change what you have always believed to be true. Your new thought will stand opposed to everything you have ever believed.

But your human spirit is attracted to pure truth no matter how much error has been planted in it. As you begin to accept these truths as being even slightly possible, your spirit will grab on that mustard-seed faith and lead you toward more truths that will correspond and validate the current one. And by this process, the casting off the elements that produced death in your body will be replaced by elements that will bring life to your body.

> *Do not conform any longer to the pattern of this world, but be transformed by the renewing of your mind. Then you will be able to test and approve what God's will is—his good and pleasing will.*
>
> —Romans 12:2

Thoughts of fear, destruction, and unnatural death are a burden to the human spirit. It prevents the immune system from serving its ultimate purpose of life, love, and health. So in order to have perfect health, we must become fully aware of God promises in regards to our health, and this knowledge can only be obtained and fully understood by reading it for ourselves and think according to his purpose. The second most important thing we must do is to become knowledgeable of the human systems process and its capabilities regarding restoration. In doing so, we will begin to acknowledge our Maker's divine order that brings forth life, love, and peace and accepts health as being a divine gift that is made available to every human being on earth. Once we have become fully persuaded in our body's ability to restore itself we can then begin to apply the basic principles of health to obtain restoration through faith in it. Faith is a spiritual law that will bring forth divine order in every area of life.

Think of all living things we share our world with. They all share the principle of life, love, and health. What separates us from animals and birds and trees is that they all live by the laws of their nature. Our human nature was created for a higher purpose. Our creative ability has formed the world we live in by the power of our thoughts therefore for, our life and our body becomes a product of our thoughts. Animals were not given the option of free thought, so they serve their purpose according to their nature. All their needs are provided for in advance in abundance, and they are equipped with the instinctive ability to obtain it. They share the law of life with us; therefore, the same resources to sustain life are available to them as to us. They are not capable of thinking thoughts of lack, poverty, or disease, so they cannot summon it to them.

If we were to think thoughts of perfect health, we will put into action the law of health governed by the law of love summoning the spirit of life. Mind has always governed the matter.

It is by our divine nature that we are driven toward the higher things in life. To say that God created sickness and distributes it among his children for some higher purpose is a lie orchestrated by the devil. If that were true, then health care would be a contradiction to God's will; therefore, it would be wrong to seek medical attention of any matter. Higher than that, since all good things come from God, the health care administration wouldn't be available.

Satan can only manipulate us by counterfeiting the truth. He uses God's love and presents it to us as twisted truth, like wicker furniture. It starts out straight but ends up twisted and that's what wickedness is.

An example would be; "God caused that car accident and killed those three people to teach you a lesson. Then Satan would appear with a scripture in hand to confirm this lie as he did with Jesus on the mountain.

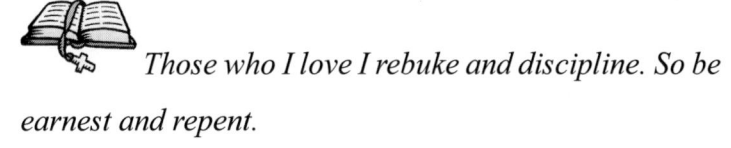

> *Those who I love I rebuke and discipline. So be earnest and repent.*
>
> —Revelation 3:19

This scripture is indeed true, but it is not parallel to this particular scenario. To rebuke is to reprimand and to discipline is to punish in order to bring correction, not death. Yes, our Creator has full authority to kill us if he so desired because after all, we belong to him; however, holy scriptures do not support that assumption. In fact, every unnatural or premature death, curse, rebuke, or destruction that took place starting with Adam, be it natural or spiritual, has occurred through the rebellion or disobedience of man. In contrary to that theory, Christ expressed the father's love for us in this parable:

> *See that you do not look down on one of these little ones. For I tell you that their angels in heaven always see the face of my Father in heaven. What do you think? If a man owns a hundred sheep, and one of them wanders away, will he not leave the ninety-nine on the hills and go to look for the one that wandered off? And if he finds it, I tell you the truth, he is happier about that one sheep than about the ninety-nine that did not wander off. In the same way your Father in heaven is not willing that any of these little ones should be lost.*
>
> —Matthew 18:10-14

Some may say, "If God loved us, why would he allow such suffering?"

I cannot proclaim to know the cause behind every kind of human suffering in the earth. There are many things that we would never know in this lifetime and will remain with God.

> *The secret things belong to God, but the things revealed belong to us and to our children forever, that we may follow all the words of the law.*
>
> —Deuteronomy 29:29

God, however, does give us a promise in Romans 8:28,

And we know that in all things God works for the good of those who love him, who have been called according to his purpose.

But there is one thing that I know without a doubt, and that is the seedtime and harvest law. We need to recognize that we ourselves are the creators of the life we live. By this I mean we make choices to live by this or by that. There are bad things happening to good people every day but it is through the will of man that people are suffering and not by the will of God himself. We have a creative nature through the spirit of God that gives us access to the spiritual realm where all created things find their origin. With every thought, word, or action, there is a law of return in motion. With every thought, we create our life in advance, and the spiritual forces of life respond to our most predominant thought. The circumstances in which we live have existed within us long before the situation presented itself. I am not by any means saying that a person can only get cancer by focusing on cancer, although that is one way of summoning this condition to oneself. What I mean to imply is sin, condemnation, and fear bring, as hosts, a myriad of effects. The spiritual law of sin is death, not necessarily eternal death, but it will bring destruction to anyone who participates in it and will take on many forms of destruction.

None of us want medical problems to occur in our lives, so we try our best to avoid the thought altogether; however, there are many who expect it to happen to them based on genetic reasoning. With these facts at hand, they go through life believing it's possible for them, and because of this, they spend their lives preparing themselves for that dreadful day and it comes as expected.

What the wicked dreads will overtake him; what the righteous desire will be granted.
—Proverbs 10:24

However, the Bible teaches us that sin and disobedience is the primary cause of all suffering.

There are only three ways to sin in this earth, and it is by thought, word, and action. And with every sin, there is a curse that's sure to follow. Seedtime and harvest functions in every area of life. Therefore, the Bible warns us mostly against false speech, evil thoughts, and sinful acts against humanity. From Adam to Revelation, there are countless examples of sin and its effects on the human nature. To my utter amazement, I have learned that evil speech is also a form of sin, which summons destruction. Here are just a few scriptures to consider regarding this fact:

📖 *The tongue also is a fire, a world of evil among the parts of the body. It corrupts the whole person, sets the whole course of his life on fire, and is itself set on fire by hell.*

—James 3:16

📖 *Their throats are open graves; their tongues practice deceit. The poison of vipers is on their lips. Their mouths are full of cursing and bitterness. Their feet are swift to shed blood; ruin and misery mark their ways.*

—Proverbs 3:13-16

📖 *He who guards his lips guards his life, but he who speaks rashly will come to ruin.*

—Proverbs 13:3

Deuteronomy 28:15 teaches us that the repercussion of sin is disease eating away at the body until it's gone. It tells us that poverty is the ruin of the poor.

There is also another fact to consider in regard to our health; God has made us to be free moral agents, free to choose what we believe, and has given us spiritual laws and principles to live by and function accordingly in this earth that will work for us or against us, making us the pilot of our life.

The reason many of us have been hindered in our knowledge in regard to the spiritual principles that govern our life can be credited back to the lack of knowledge of our parents. "A tree is known by its fruit." We cannot give what we do not have; therefore, in many cases our children are sent into the world as clueless as a newborn, placed in a dangerous environment, left to fend for itself.

We have become so *"earthly"* that until recently we were literally uninformed and incorrect about everything pertaining to life. Spirit, soul, and body as a unit were of no importance to most of us when in truth, they are everything.

We have in error perceive our spirit as something used for eternity purposes only, and we measured our soul to be secondary to our human nature. And because of this, we develop our cravings of our flesh alone, living by our human nature, so we think.

The problem is, like Adam and Eve, in ignorance of these spiritual laws, when they work against us, we blame God by claiming that he had the power to prevent it altogether, not realizing that we summoned many conditions of life to ourselves.

Adam also blamed God then Eve for his act of sin.

> *Adam said, the woman <u>you put here</u> with me—<u>she gave me</u> some fruit from the tree and I ate it.*
> —Genesis 3:12

Adam did not look at the cause of the matter either; he focused his attention to the act as if that's where it started. Before this, Adam did not sin. He was perfect in the eyes of God. Nonetheless, he was held responsible for the sin even though Eve initiated it. This is because God gave *Adam* a direct order not to eat of the tree and told *him* what would happen if he did not obey. All this was established before Eve was created. But because he rebelled against the law of life, he was thrown out of the garden along with Eve, having hindered himself from the benefit of a pure and upright life. In addition to this, through his sin, he was made unrighteous in the sight of God, so because the entire human race was within Adam's loins at the time of his sin, we were all born into his unrighteous state of being into the law of sin and death.

What we must come to realize is God is bound by the integrity of his word. He cannot and will not violate the spiritual principle he put in place to govern the earth, just as the justice system will not violate its laws for the likes of one man although there are many occasions that will prove contrary, which clearly prove that we can never measure up to the integrity of God.

Adam disobeyed God before he was taught of these spiritual laws from the tree of knowledge, causing a curse to enter into the life of man. But then Jesus came to cancel the curse of death and to demonstrate for us our true identity in God and declared *"by faith, we will do as he has done and even more things than this."* He denied no one this power or gift of life. During his healing ministry, he asked no questions as to why one was sick and afflicted nor did he look to genetics for reasoning. For him, being the living spirit of God himself, knowing the cause behind every effect, never having to separate one cause from another, he simply said as he healed the sick

See, you are well again. Stop sinning or something worse may happen to you.

—John 5:14

Some men brought to him a paralytic, lying on a mat. When Jesus saw their faith, he said to the paralytic, "Take heart, son; your sins are forgiven." At this, some of the teachers of the law said to themselves,

> *"This fellow is blaspheming!" Knowing their thoughts, Jesus said, "Why do you entertain evil thoughts in your hearts? Which is easier: to say, 'Your sins are forgiven,' or to say, 'Get up and walk'? But so that you may know that the Son of Man has authority on earth to forgive sins . . ." Then he said to the paralytic, "Get up, take your mat and go home." And the man got up and went home.*

You see, sin has no face but takes on many forms. Though it may be true a person did not ever think of having a particular disease, yet the reason they may have it is because when we are not equipped with the full knowledge of God and the armor he advises us to use against the evil forces of this world described in Ephesians 6:13, we are unprotected therefore vulnerable to the evil forces of this world.

> *When an evil spirit comes out of a man, it goes through arid places seeking rest and does not find it. Then it says, "I will return to the house I left." When it arrives, it finds the house unoccupied, swept clean and put in order. Then it goes and takes with it seven other spirits more wicked than itself, and they go in and live there. And the final condition of that man is worse than the first. That is how it will be with this wicked generation.*
>
> —Matthew 12:43-45

This scripture teaches us that we must keep our guard up at all times against the evils of this world. The moment we begin to think that we have nothing to worry about, is the unguarded door that Satan uses to gain access into our lives.

When we become saved, our spirits are transformed from death to life with Christ. We become shielded in him, redeemed from the curse of spiritual death. Our physical bodies however remain subjected to death afforded by our sinful nature. Sin has serious consequences for us in our human nature and we will suffer those consequences.

There will be trouble and distress for every human being who does evil.

—Romans 2:9

This is a matter of spirit versus flesh. Although we have a sinful nature, it does not mean that we should live by it. We all can live and should live according to the spirit, which is, in hindsight, God's intended purpose to begin with.

Therefore, there is now no condemnation for those who are in Christ Jesus, because through Christ Jesus the law of the Spirit of life set me free from the law

> *of sin and death. For what the law was powerless to do in that it was weakened by the sinful nature, God did by sending his own Son in the likeness of sinful man to be a sin offering. And so he condemned sin in sinful man, in order that the righteous requirements of the law might be fully met in us, who do not live according to the sinful nature but according to the Spirit.*
>
> *Those who live according to the sinful nature have their minds set on what that nature desires; but those who live in accordance with the Spirit have their minds set on what the Spirit desires. The mind of sinful man is death, but the mind controlled by the Spirit is life and peace; the sinful mind is hostile to God. It does not submit to God's law, nor can it do so. Those controlled by the sinful nature cannot please God.*
>
> —Romans 8:1-8

Spiritual laws are more solid than any natural law you live by on this earth. Spiritual laws will forever be the same from now till eternity while natural laws are temporal and will perish with the earth.

We function within the karma law, the law of return. We will most certainly reap what we sow, good or bad. Every day with every thought there is a spiritual law operating in our lives, working for us or against us, and God will not go against the laws he created to govern our lives, but through faith in him and his word, he will demonstrate his powers through us by causing us to overcome any adversity by faith.

There are many sick and afflicted people who believe that God can deliver them from their troubles. But the problem is they refuse to believe that he has given them the ability through Christ in their spirit to break free from the thing that has enslaved them.

While they are waiting for him to do something for them, he is waiting on them to use what he has freely given to them by his grace, which is the power to command by faith. The Holy Spirit that's within us relies on your faith in its ability to manifest the goodness of God. He's given to us the power through spiritual laws and provisions to overcome all things in this physical world and to change the circumstances surrounding us.

> *His divine power has given us everything we need for life and godliness through our knowledge of him who called us by his own glory and goodness.*
> —2 Peter 1:3

If we can begin to increase our knowledge in regard to the promises God has made through his covenant of peace and begin to focus our attention on the provisions that he has made through his Spirit and not on the problem itself, it will cause us to focus on the love of God and perfect health will, by the law of return, come as a result. Then our life will, by spiritual law, operate in the love of God, and disease can never remain in a body governed by a healthy mind.

The spiritual realms of life have no physical form, so it's impossible for God to think disease, discord, or deficiency; if he did, we would have been created from a self-destructive force. God is eternal and can never be destroyed, neither can our spirit.

Satan, however, is the god of destruction, and he deals with us according to our physical nature. He cannot touch our human spirit because it is of God, but he is more than willing to assist us in the destruction of our souls. All physical disorders are impure, man-made thoughts that can only affect human nature. God is not responsible for our shortcomings, we are. He does not dwell in the physical realm, we do. We summon these physical conditions on ourselves by unconsciously rejecting the law of health.

They have darkened their understanding and separated themselves from the life of God because of the ignorance that is in them due to the hardening of their hearts. Having lost all sensitivity, they have given themselves over to sensuality so as to indulge in every kind of impurity with a continual lust for more.

-Ephesians 4: 18-19

This Particular scripture takes the blame off of God and places our destruction back into our own hands. We darken our understanding by rejecting his word. By this our thought life remains worldly, and becomes more and more receptive to the ways of the world and so we ourselves become a by-product of this fallen world.

It is because of this we have separated ourselves from the life that God intended for us to have. God further explains that it is because of our lack of knowledge of him that we have separated ourselves due to the hardening of our hearts. God explains that it is our lack of sensitivity to our way of life that is not only responsible for our separation, but our destruction as well.

This lack of sensitivity enables us to participate in the sinful ways of this world; murder, strife, rage, anger, sexual immorality of every kind, unforgivingness, slander and every other kind of evil, all this without conscience or remorse.

God has crated us all with individual purposes. But just as he gave the angels in heaven free will to serve along with the first man on earth the freedom of choice, so it is with us.

> *This day i call heaven and earth as witnesses against you that i have set before you life and death, blessings and curses. NOW choose life so that you and your children may live.*
>
> -deuteronomy 30:15

In the following chapters you will find some very interesting facts regarding health and healing. You will learn health is a condition of the mind and that God never intended for us to live a life of calamity, discord, or error. You will come to understand that the renewal of your mind is critical to your well-being.

Mind over Matter

It is a proven fact through the life we live that the law of health is always at work within us to bring us perfect health. Our human spirit is there to develop your health and lead us into the will of God, but it needs our mind as an aid to assist in the process; therefore, it is absolutely imperative that we think according to the nature of absolute health.

> *What the wicked dreads will overtake him; what the righteous desire will be granted.*
>
> —Proverbs 10:24

I find it necessary to reiterate the foundation of my message to you that you may consider this central point in regards to health. Your soul is made up of your mind, emotions, and your will. Your imagination lies within your mind. It's called the inner eye, the eye that can see the things that are not present to the naked eye. All of these play a major role in the development of a person and is responsible for their success or failure. But the human spirit is the beginning of it all. It's the very reason we exist.

The human spirit will develop any thoughts, words, or images we entertain. This is why one day's trouble is different from the next. When we clean up one mess, there's another awaiting our attention. With each passing thought, word, or action in association with fear, which is a negative form of faith, it produces corresponding circumstances of worry for tomorrow. We are constantly recreating our life's order in harmony with our thoughts. When we think, we create; in doing so we are ordering tomorrow's events in advance and those who are unaware of spiritual laws do this unconsciously.

In this state of flowing, unmanaged thoughts, unexpected events will arrive correspondent to its nature of thought, and due to a persons lack of knowledge regarding this matter, they will remain in total darkness in regards to life and the circumstances that surround it.

Christians who are aware of the power of right thought and words are always in a constant battle with the flesh by consciously ordering thoughts of the things desired and casting down the unfavorable one. Yes, it is a very brutal exercise. But those whose thoughts and words are not measured and chosen carefully, their lives are like a wave in the sea. They will find that their lives have drifted off to a far-off place, and once arriving at that place, they will never understand how it ended up there. It's the same as falling asleep on a bus, oblivious to the things that took place during the ride.

Negative thoughts find their origin in fear. So when negative thoughts enter the domain of the mind, those thought currents are passed to the domain of the human spirit to produce according to its nature.

The spirit does not determine the nature of the seed; it only knows to develop what's been planted in it.

The good man brings good things out of the good stored up in him, and the evil man brings evil things out of the evil stored up in him.

—Matthew 12:25

By this scripture we now understand that with every thought, word or deed, we are storing up within ourselves good or evil. Whatever we give our attention to the most is what is being panted within us.

Negative thinking is toxic thoughts releasing the toxic elements of its kind into your body, and your spirit was created to work for you, to obey your will, and develop according to your mind-set. The way we live, the things we experience in our state of health are all a manifestation of what we believe and pay attention to.

Things such as disease, death, addiction, jealousy, hatred, depression, joy, peace, sadness, pain, and lust do not have the ability to manifest into objective forms, so they become conditions of the mind, and when these conditions are expressed in either word or thought, the body responds and becomes one with the condition. The body will always be present with the condition of the mind.

If you can recall past thoughts of anger, rage, or jealousy, you could feel the effects in your body; your blood begins to rush and the heart rate rapidly increases as you become more engaged in the thought. This is proof of the body being present with the condition of your mind. These emotions also trigger our glands to respond, so in our rage we sweat, tear up, or get dry mouth. These emotions will also cause anxiety proving that these particular conditions of the mind have the ability to affect our nervous system. The entire human nature is affected in any emotional state, and so the body is forced to work harder than it was created to.

Now if your mind can trigger that kind of effect on your body, creating a stressful environment within your human nature, wouldn't it be sensible to accept that the damage that has been done to the body as a result of those mental conditions, is a direct reflection of what a person hold in their mind? Just imagine thinking and feeling those bad emotions regularly, although your spirit was designed to repair the body with sleep, how could it if you went to bed with those thoughts, woke up with those same thoughts, and took your body to the battlefield consistently?

Your body also responds to other forms of thinking such as sadness, lust, or laughter. If a person was to tell you someone you loved had died, that mental image will trigger your emotions, and your emotions will cause you to cry and be in distress. When we lust over someone in our mind, the thought will put into motion a number of physical responses that involves our muscles, glands, and blood prompting us to physically carry it out. In regard to laughter, words spoken in good humor or the thought of something funny will cause our abdominal muscles to jerk in uncontrolled laughter. By these things we know that our bodies are always present with the condition of the mind. My body is a slave to my mind. As you can now see, all these mental conditions have to, by law, manifest itself into physical form as all things do.

But a heart and mind that's geared toward negativity can have a deadly effect on the body. When you entertain evil thoughts in your heart, you will become a bitter person who lives in hatred toward others. Those are very strong emotions that will consume your every thought. As your body continues to work hard to create a peaceful environment for itself, it will in time become weary and weak, never having the time to fight off your germ-manifested thoughts. They come at a rapid pace attaching to it more like elements such as deceit, strife, unforgiveness, and revenge. And because of these thoughts, peace is far from you. The mind creates stressful conditions in the body, which causes trauma to your organs, the end result being stress-related illnesses that will weaken the immune system and eventually lead to disease and/or unnatural death of some kind.

Try listening to the testimony of one or two people who are sick. You would see that their words line up with their physical ailment. You will also notice that as they confirm their present state of injury, they will also establish the possible hardship that lies ahead. But don't let their testimony mislead you. These conditions did not just fall on their lap one morning; they summoned it to them by making it a possibility in their life long before it showed up by either speaking about the possibility or by living a life of strife and resentment, or it could be that there was a gate left unguarded where the enemy has slipped in unnoticed as I mentioned previously. But if none of those mind sets apply to you, then what does not belong to you will not stay with you. God does not promise any of us a peaceful ride through earth. But he does promise to clear a path for us through the wilderness. Sickness cannot remain in a healthy state of mind.

It's never wise to believe that everything just happens. If that were truly the case, then we would have no other choice but to accept the situation and live with it, and if we take on that view of life in its totality, then we're all screwed because this world is full of suffering, and in most cases, when it rains it pours. That kind of mind-set leads to hopelessness.

Many of us would rather believe that our circumstances just happened out of nowhere but say in the same breath "everything happens for a reason."

That's a fair statement when applied to someone else's life. Such people would say, "diabetes, cancer or hypertension runs in my family so I will most likely develop theses conditions as well."

Since early childhood, they were taught that these ailments were a possibility for them genetically so they begin to accept this fate as a future reality and failure. After years of considering these issues, their mind becomes conditioned in the possibility. Faith is developed in their fear, so those conditions must show up by the spiritual law of *seedtime and harvest*.

> *What the wicked dreads will overtake him; what the righteous desire will be granted.*
> —Proverbs 10:24

> *What I feared has come upon me; what I dreaded has happened to me. I have no peace, no quietness; I have no rest, but only turmoil.*
> —Job 3:25-26

The curse that operates in my family is cervical cancer and hypertension. I never once considered it; therefore, it does not pertain to me. Even if Satan tries to present it to me by presenting the evidence in my body, I will not own up to it.

When we begin to accept affliction of any kind as a way of life and death, that thought current must correlate with the nature of its kind and so we attract these conditions to ourselves through faith in it. The cure for any illness lies with a persons knowledge of their ability to think perfect health, having faith in the promises of God regarding health and to know in absolute truth that your spirit will develop the desired condition. These are the weapons we were equipped with for spiritual warfare. That's our power. It's faith in the love and goodness of the Almighty God.

Your Body, behind Enemy Lines

Understand that your body is the battlefield of your mind, and its present condition is the result of your war. With every thought that's accompanied by an emotion, it takes on a physical form of some kind whether it is good or bad. Good thoughts promote peaceful conditions with the human system and bad thoughts will develop a stressful environment. But know that every evil thought is sent out as a real force whether it is of hatred, anger, deceit, or jealousy. Every evil thought that you send forth to harm another human being will return to you by the spiritual law of return and do its greatest work in you. But understand that sickness should not always be viewed as an unfortunate ailment, for there are great benefits that derive through sickness.

It is by the law of life that the body repairs itself through sickness. But sickness has always been accompanied by fear of physical discomfort or death, and our subconscious mind confirms it through past experiences of others. But if we remain unwilling to change our thinking habits, our mind will continue to store these dreaded memories for a lifetime, and it's these kinds of thought patterns that hinders the healing process altogether.

Every time we get sick, Satan is there to confirm our adversity in fear, adding to it every kind of false belief, and out of our mouth from our hearts comes the words to establish this end result by saying "I feel like I'm dying" or "This cold is killing me" or "I knew I was going to get this."

Our body was created to respond and repair the natural conditions of human nature. The brain was designed to signal the body to destroy any undesired element that enters the body. It also prompts the body to repair itself. But the human will has the ability to over ride the healing ability of the human system therefore, our body is constantly changing with the condition of our minds, and with constant demolition of the human body caused by evil thoughts, these forces throw the natural functions of our entire body off course, causing it to function under very stressful conditions by taking in more than it can give.

> *The tongue also is a fire, a world of evil among the parts of the body. It corrupts the whole person, sets the whole course of his life on fire, and is itself set on fire by hell.*
> —James 3:16

By the law of return, most commonly known as karma, our expressed thoughts of defeat within our own lives or that of ill will or harm toward others belong to us, and so they return to us. And it is by the law of growth that they attach to them on their journey, elements of destruction, returning to us a hundredfold.

Since our physical nature is weak in comparison to the powerful forces of this world, after a period of time, the effects become physically obvious; the thoughts take form in our bodies. It causes a change in our physique, hair, and blood. It also affects the pigmentation of the skin, causing one to look as if they are worn out, as they truly are. The result of this raging battle within you is stress. Stress in your body is trauma to your organs, and this too shall take form by way of death.

But death doesn't always have to take its stand. If we can learn to change our thinking, we can most certainly change the course of our life.

> *Do not conform any longer to the pattern of this world, but <u>be transformed by the renewing of your mind</u>. Then you will be able to test and approve what God's will is—<u>his good, pleasing and perfect</u> will is.*
>
> —Romans 12:2

> *He who guards his lips guards his life, but he who speaks rashly will come to ruin.*
>
> —Proverbs 13:3

Because we have formed so many bad habits, it'll cost us some time and discomfort in order for restoration to come, but we must summon it to us by the highest law, the law of love, and by this we must understand that before things get better, they get a lot worse. Relief is not always immediate, but it is definite no matter the damage. It's a promise from God.

> *They cried to the Lord in their trouble, and he saved them from their distress. He sent forth his word and healed them, he rescued them from the grave.*
> —Psalms 107:20

In addition to this, we were also commanded to love thy neighbor as we love ourself. This is a commandment of love. It's an order, not an option. We were born to a self-destructive nature, and by this commandment, we escape the grips of death. God's good and perfect will is hidden in this commandment, and his mercy and grace is the engine of which it arrived.

Metamorphosis: Out with the Old, in with the New

New thoughts bring new life. The road to self-healing is established through the calling of health and strength to drive out disease. But we cannot obtain the best health without changing the way we think. What we see and what we grow up believing have a huge influence over what we accept to be true in our lives. By replacing thoughts of hate with thoughts of love, our spirit magically although gradually replace the bad with the good. If it can find one pure, healthy thought to build on, it's like a narrow, open doorway in which it can attach to itself more like truths expanding its entry for the good. Good and evil cannot dwell in the same setting. One has to go, but understand that your body will suffer the battle.

> *Therefore, since Christ suffered in his body, arm yourselves with the same attitude, because he who has suffered in his body is done with sin. As a result, he does not live the rest of his earthly life for evil desires, but rather for the will of God.*
>
> —1 Peter 4:1

We must prepare our minds for the hard work and suffering that's involved in the changing process. For if our minds are prepared for the challenge and our eyes are on the prize to come, then hope is established, which is the beginning of faith, and by faith, change will reach its fullness and give us more life.

Change not only produces sanctification, but it's our spirits way of prioritizing our life. Change gets rid of dead matter in the body, and our spirit brings new life to all areas of the human system.

Most people dread illness. They accept it as a form of death. Whether it shows up in the form of a common cold, fever, or flu, we have been trained to reject it and to do all we can to prevent it from taking form in our bodies. Little do know that by this, we do more harm to ourselves than good.

In order to be free of any life-threatening ailment, we must first understand why it's there, that the problem is not within the form of sickness itself, but the cause behind the sickness. Sickness in the body is the result of a spiritual war within your mind. It's only a physical manifestation of the evil that's stored within the human heart.

> *For our struggle is not against flesh and blood, but against the rulers, against the authorities, against the powers of this dark world and against the spiritual forces of evil in the heavenly realms.*
> —Ephesians 6:12

It is impossible to kill a plant by cutting it down; we must destroy the root because by cutting it down, it will reproduce. The same thing is true where our health is concerned. It is impossible to kill a disease by suppressing or fighting the bacteria but by destroying the cause, the germinating thought pattern that summoned it to begin with. It is a spiritual issue, a war that exceeds far beyond our own understanding, created in the spiritual realms of life. But the spirit within is equipped to handle such a battle. Our job is not to conquer the disease in our own strength through man made drugs because that only has temporary benefits, but to familiarize ourselves with the nature of our human spirit and its strength and purpose if we could ever hope to conquer it all together.

Colds, coughs, fevers, aches, and pains are caused by the spiritual process of restoration. Our spirit was designed to reconstruct our body by casting off the old and dead matter and replacing it with new life. In this process, we become fatigued, unable to function due to the war going on in our bodies. As you know, when we get sick, we have little or nothing at all to do with the rejuvenation of our bodies. We may think we're contributing to our health by taking some form of medication because it was created to fight the bacteria that put the human body in distress; however, if you really think about it, the cold, flu, fever, aches, and pain will all pass through without our help. The medication is there only to ease the side effects as an aid that can only assist the spirit temporarily as it repairs its vessel. In truth, drugs actually hinders and in many cases destroy the bodies ability to heal due to the unnatural substance that medications are produced with. Although they were created with good intentions, to destroy the bad bacteria or cells, they also destroy the good bacteria and cells along with the bad ones. For this reason, our immune system becomes weak within its ability to restore, causing a person to become totally reliant on drugs in order to maintain some minimal level of comfort and total destruction of the human system becomes an end result.

As every living thing in this earth reconstructs itself by the casting out of the old to bring in the new, so do we, but our casting off shows up in the form of physical discomfort and temporary illness through our blood and organs.

As you can see, all living things go through the painful process of change, and all forms of change has its price to pay, some more than others.

A caterpillar takes a journey from the dirt to the trees and cocoons itself in order to receive its new body. An eagle, the king of the air, when its being renewed, loses all its feathers including its beak. When this process takes place, it hides within the crevices of a mountain due to its lack of strength becoming prey itself. You can also see this amazing process in nature itself such as the rain forests and its mighty wonders of self-destruction, replenishing, rejuvenation, beauty, abundance, and life.

Since we're thinking beings, our bodies are constantly changing its elements with the conditions of our mind. The things we fear are being set up for us in advance, and the evil we do in thought is being developed in our bodies.

Let's use a car as an example to this fact. When the battery dies, we don't give in to the problem by doing away with the entire car. We buy another battery. In fact, with every breakdown, we assess the problem and make the necessary repairs, never accepting its malfunction. If only we assessed our health issues with the same wisdom.

This is how we make our physical ailment worse: we say, "I hate being sick or I wish I didn't have the flu." Because our body is a direct reflection of our mind, by this we are telling our immune system and spirit to "back off, I don't want you working on my behalf!" And since the power that governs our entire body is in our mind and is established through our mouth, every atom, cell, tissue, and organ has to, by law, obey the command by backing off. When the mind is full of defeat, our words declare it; therefore, our bodies follow suit.

In this state of mind, our body has no defense. It's been abandoned by the spirit because the human spirit was created to work with the mind, which is a counterpart of the soul. It's at this point that we become spiritually dead. As decay runs its course, death is inevitable.

For who among men knows the thoughts of a man except the man's spirit within him? In the same way no one knows the thoughts of God except the Spirit of God.

<u>We have not received the spirit of the world but the Spirit who is from God, that we may understand what God has freely given us.</u> This is what we speak, not in words taught us by human wisdom but in words taught by the Spirit, expressing spiritual truths in spiritual words. The man without the Spirit does not accept the things that come from the Spirit of God, for they are foolishness to him, and he cannot understand them, because they are spiritually discerned.

—1 Corinthians 2:11-14

In order to get well, we must think according to the nature and the purpose of the spirit, and when this is done, the human spirit responds and restoration begins.

If we are to ever achieve complete restoration of our bodies, we need to begin looking at disease as a result of some form of sin and the physical discomfort as a result of a spiritual process that our bodies must go through in order for us to become healthy again.

Our thoughts manifest itself into form through our flesh and blood, and through discomfort, our spirit drives it out, providing it's properly and carefully fed thoughts and words of spiritual encouragement.

Any hateful thoughts that are sent out against another human being are in violation of the law of love; therefore, they find their origin in sin, and scripture clearly teaches us that the wages of sin is death. So it is imperative that we understand that these emotions create disorder within our bodies. They corrupt our spirit and destroy our human nature by manifesting into forms of decay and does just as much harm over time as any indigestible food, drug, or alcohol-based substance. These emotions are created in the mind. Since the mind finds its origin in the soul and the soul the spirit, which is the sum total of our entire creative nature, anything created from it goes out as a spiritual force to create according to the nature of the thought.

Since bad thoughts can never take on an objective form in the world or in another person, they must demonstrate their creative ability within the host that sent it. This truth is confirmed in us with every bad emotion while the person to whom they were directed at will not lose one minute's rest. Our thoughts become our own.

If all of these biblical quotes are true, "seedtime and harvest will never cease, a man will reap what he sow, as a man thinks in his heart so he is, words have the power of life and death," then it is no mystery as to why God made love a commandment, not an option. This commandment safeguards the ignorant from self-imposed destruction *if* we *will* obey it.

It is impossible to drive out disease so long as we're feeding it through these sin-based emotions. It's the same as eating too many of the wrong foods. When we consume them at a rapid pace, too quick for the body to burn it, the indigestible foods are stored as fat that will eventually lead to major health issues. That's our system operating under a stressful environment, becoming unable to produce health. The same is true regarding the spirit of life.

But if we can begin to manage our thoughts, rightly order them in advance, our attitude toward life would change for the future and become a direct reflection of what we hold inside. Health then becomes inevitable and must manifest itself by the law of love. Love is life.

By this spiritual renewal of the body, each time our mind accepts the truth of any matter, it causes a disappearance of the false belief in the other matter. This is called the law of compensation. What you gain in one area, you lose in the next. Light will always cause the disappearance of darkness.

With each new thought of truth, it causes a casting off the old untruth (dead matter), which has in the past materialized in your body. And as a result, the body suffers for a time but restoration is at hand.

> *So I say live by the spirit and you will not gratify the desires of the sinful nature, for the sinful nature desires what is contrary to the spirit and the spirit what is contrary to the sinful nature. They are in conflict with each other so that you do not know what you want.*
>
> —Galatians 4:16

Let me give you a scenario, picture the truth as "love" and the false belief "hate." Love and hate go to battle. Love wants to give you life and hate wants to take it away. You decide you want to live, so love conquers hate and destroys it. It's now left in the field to die. The body is the dumping ground for your thoughts.

It's a spiritual graveyard. The spirit, by law, has to repair the vessel of which it dwells that it may bring forth the life God intended for us to have.

A human system polluted by death is the result of a sick spirit. However, a healthy spirit desires to live in a healthy environment, and it is for this reason that we decide to choose life that the rejuvenated spirit goes to work by rebuilding his house.

Therefore, if anyone is in Christ, he is a new creation; the old has gone, the new has come.
—2 Corinthians 5:17

You were taught, with regard to your former way of life, to put off your old self, which is being corrupted by its deceitful desires; <u>to be made new in the attitude of your minds</u> and to put on the new self, created to be like God in true righteousness and holiness.
—Ephesians 4:20-24

In order for new life to come in, the old has to be pushed out the way. We see this principle operating in everything. With our children, in order for new teeth to come in, the old teeth have to go. In nature, everything dies and is given new life in due season. Snakes shed their skin, animals shed their fur, and so on. But we cast off deadly elements of decay through sickness.

Your belief will make your sickness a benefit or an evil to your body. If you think according to your spirit and view your sickness as a spiritual process for getting you well, your mind becomes an aid to your spirit and you then contribute to the healing of your body. But if you dread being sick and curse the process, in doing so you stop the process of liberation by silently telling your immune system to shut down and your spirit to back off. Remember, your body and your spirit responds to the conditions of your mind.

Truth will always reveal a lie. Love will always overcome hate as light will always destroy darkness. After being ruled with negative thoughts and emotions for so long, with right thoughts your spirit will now return to its original position as being the dominant force of life, love, and health in you and attract to it all the elements that bring health, and you will be, in the end, healthy without a trace of your past ailment. This is because you have placed yourself in the position to receive it by coming to a place of complete submission to the spirit of God, trusting it and getting familiar with its mission.

Have nothing to do with godless myths and old wives' tales; rather, train yourself to be godly; For physical training is of some value, but godliness has value for all things, holding promise for both the present life and the life to come. This is a trustworthy saying that deserves full acceptance (and for this we labor and strive), that we have put our hope in the living God, who is the Savior of all men and especially of those who believe.

—1 Timothy 4:7-10

Now if you choose to believe that sickness is in its totality a physical condition, not a spiritual process that drives out disease but that no good can come from it, only pain, suffering, and ultimately unnatural death, your body will come into agreement with your mind and you will in truth be defeated at every turn.

This is the reason the body parts we hate the most, whether it be a failed organ or a cosmetic issue, will always appear to be one of our biggest physical problems. It can never get well or become pleasing to our eyes because we have rejected it, dismissed it, and accepted the death of it. This is especially true for those who suffer from organ disease.

It is impossible to be of benefit to the healing process of any kind in despising the part that's sick. Our bodily organs work together as a unit, and when one part fails, it affects the whole system just as everything else in life. We can become a huge benefit to our bodies through love and encouragement even when it's sick. You wouldn't despise a loved one for being sick, would you? Of course not, you would nurse them back to health with love no matter what the damage because they are a part of you.

So it is with our body. We cannot just do away with it when it becomes sick; we nurse it back to health by talking to it and feeding it properly with words of encouragement and love until it's able to stand strong in its place and rejoin the forces that bring us life. Life is a precious gift from God, and he desires that we live long and strong. TLC has always been the best medicine because it's a regimen formulated by God. The spirit was created to carry out our thoughts and words. Complete restoration comes through words of encouragement, words of love.

> *Do not conform any longer to the pattern of this world, but be transformed by the renewing of your mind. Then you will be able to test and approve what God's will is—his good, pleasing and perfect will.*
>
> —Romans 12:2

Restoration

Without sickness, we cannot get well, and sickness is brought out into physical form through our immune system working perfectly as it should. The human nature was created to warn us through sickness of a possible dangerous atmosphere that is taking place within our system. Our vitals change dramatically when something is going wrong. This is our cue to either seek medical attention or to pray in faith, and it is by these signs that we know that our bodies are working as they should.

Now I'm not suggesting that you should praise the very thing that can possibly cause you great harm. What I mean by this is when we get sick, instead of focusing on the hurt, we ought to acknowledge the law of life working within us, know with confidence that we are getting better, and by this, we create a mental atmosphere of faith in our restoration.

We ought to praise our immune system and spirit for functioning perfectly according to its purpose by getting rid of all germ-manifested thoughts that encourage the diseases to destroy our bodies. By having confidence in this process, it will build your faith in its purpose and healing will come.

You have to know that your spirit is the production center for your life, that the harvest of your garden represents a seed sown into your life. You have to understand that your body cannot live its full, intended purpose without your mind acting as its aid by thinking in line with its purpose.

Whenever I get a cold or cough, I thank and give praise to God that my immune system is functioning properly and confess that healing is on the way. This not only increases my faith, but it also keeps my mind focused on the power that God has created me with. Whenever I feel the need to take medication, I confess that I am only taking this as an aid to my spirit to bring me temporary relief as my spirit brings new life to my body. By this I take hold of the grace given me and leave all the glory for God.

I have learned to embrace the spirit of life that dwells within the members of my body by acknowledging its purpose as being the dominate source of my being. I have also learned to respect my body as a unit, by acknowledging its functions as a whole, and having faith in its purpose. I never confess to being sick, knowing that my health is at stake and is established through faith in my words. I just thank God for my healing and ability to overcome any adversity.

> *The tongue has the power of life and death, and those who love it will eat its fruit.*
>
> —Proverbs 18:21

> *This day I call heaven and earth as witnesses against you that I have set before you life and death, blessings and curses. Now choose life, so that you and your children may live.*
>
> —Deuteronomy 30:19

Chapter 10

An illustration from Job

What I feared has come upon me; what I dreaded has happened to me.

—Job 3:25

Job was considered blameless in the sight of God and man. He was very wealthy, having been blessed by God for his loyalty and prospered in everything he put his hands on, resulting in total life prosperity. He had seven sons and three daughters. His story teaches us that he feared God and shunned evil. In this scripture, you may see that Job did no wrong. But that can't be true because he lost everything and all his children died at once. Well, what did Job do that deserved total destruction of his life? Chapter *1:4-5* explains his sin.

> *His sons used to take turns holding feasts in their homes, and they would invite their three sisters to eat and drink with them. When a period of feasting had run its course,*

Job would send and have them purified. Early in the morning he would sacrifice a burnt offering for each of them, <u>thinking, "Perhaps my children have sinned and cursed God in their hearts." This was Job's regular custom.</u>

Although he loved God, he thought negatively about his children and feared their destruction.

> *What I feared has come upon me; what I dreaded has happened to me.*
>
> —Job 3:25

Notice how the fear took place in his heart before the destruction appeared in his life. He operated in fear regularly because verse 5 concludes that it was his *regular custom* to sacrifice burnt offerings to God to purify his children of the sins they may have never committed. He was led by his fear, and his fear became his destruction. He was calling things that are not as though they were.

Although God knew Job loved him, he knew the destruction Job summoned to himself and his family by the law of fear. Since Satan is the lord over fear, he hearkens to the voice of it.

> Then the Lord said to Satan, "Have you considered my servant Job? There is no one on earth like him; he is blameless and upright, a man who fears God and shuns evil."
>
> —Job 1:8

In this statement, it's apparent that Job summoned the angels of darkness to him by his thoughts and actions. It's fair to say this because Satan would not have *considered* pursuing Job as a prime candidate for destruction if he was living by faith in the love of God.

Fear is a powerful force, a spiritual law that will bring the thing feared to you. When Satan went about to cause his destruction upon Job, he was unable to touch him due to the hedge of protection God placed around him.

> "Does Job fear God for nothing?" Satan replied. <u>"Have you not put a hedge around him and his household and everything he has?</u> You have blessed the work of his hands, so that his flocks and herds are spread throughout the land. But stretch out your hand and strike everything he has, and he will surely curse you to your face."
>
> —Job 1:9-11

Satan and his angels appeared to God to accuse Job of his sin, demanding their right to destroy the things feared as God ordained as spiritual law before time. He also accused Job of being faithful to God due to his wealth.

Because faith and fear are two powerful forces, one governed by God and the other by Satan, God would not go back on his word and what he established in this earth. But he will intercede by his grace, which is what he did for Job prior to his destruction. Also, take note that Satan is showing his inferiority to God, acknowledging that God is the ultimate power of this world. He does this by acknowledging that all his power lies in the hands of God, which is the reason he said, "Stretch out your hand and strike everything he has." He was petitioning the authority of God to peruse Job, if he would allow it, but at the same time demanding what's rightfully his, fear itself. Had God not protected Job by his grace, Satan and his angels would have had their way with him long ago. So God gave Satan permission to take everything he had except his life. Keep in mind that Job feared losing everything he had; in doing so, Satan had spiritual authority over those things.

The Lord said to Satan, "Very well, then, everything he has is in your hands, but on the man himself do not lay a finger." Then Satan went out from the presence of the Lord.

—Job 1:12

The story concludes that although Job feared losing everything he loved to evil, he never feared Satan taking his life because he knew without reservation that it belonged to God. He never cursed God for his loss as Satan suggested; instead, he took the blame upon himself, having realized his offense. In all this, God turned his ear to Job as he accepted the destruction that was upon his life, proclaiming God to be Lord over all life, having the right to strike it if so desired. This is why God considered him a blameless and upright man. After total destruction had taken over Job, he was restored to his righteous state and was given twice as much as he lost. Understand that this story has nothing to do with God proving his authority to Satan. That was already established when God threw him out of heaven and again when Satan presented his request to strike. Nor was this a power struggle. Why would a creator struggle for power with a created thing? No, this story serves as an example of faith and fear.

The book of Job serves as a good example of faith and fear.

Healing Scriptures

By faith in the name of Jesus, this man whom you see and know was made strong. It is in Jesus' name and the <u>faith </u>that comes through him that has given this <u>complete healing to him, as you can all see.</u>

—Acts 3:16

But he was pierced for our transgressions, he was crushed for our iniquities; the punishment that brought us peace was upon him, and by his wounds <u>we are healed</u>.

—Isaiah 53:5

Jesus went throughout Galilee, teaching in their synagogues, preaching the good news of the kingdom, <u>and healing every disease and sickness among the people.</u>

—Matthew 4:23

Pleasant words are a honeycomb, sweet to the soul and <u>healing to the bones</u>.

—Proverbs 16:24

But I will <u>restore you to health and heal your wounds</u>, declares the Lord.

—Jeremiah 30:17

If my people, who are called by my name, will humble themselves and pray and seek my face and turn from their wicked ways, then will I hear from heaven and will forgive their sin and <u>will heal their land</u>

—2 Chronicles 7:14

Reckless words pierce like a sword, but the tongue of the wise brings healing.

—Proverbs 12:18

Blessed is he who has regard for the weak; the Lord delivers him in times of trouble. The Lord <u>will sustain him on his sickbed and restore him from his bed of illness.</u>

—Psalm 41:1, 3

Is it not to share your food with the hungry and to provide the poor wanderer with shelter—when you see *the naked, to clothe him, and not to turn away from your own flesh and blood? <u>Then your light will break forth like the dawn, and your healing will quickly appear;</u> then your righteousness will go before you, and the glory of the Lord will be your rear guard.*

—Isaiah 58:7-8

Therefore confess your sins to each other and pray for each other <u>so that you may be healed. The prayer of a righteous man is powerful and effective</u>

—James 5:16

And in the church God has appointed first of all apostles, second prophets, third teachers, then workers of miracles, <u>also those having gifts of healing</u>, those able to help others, those with gifts of administration, and those speaking in different kinds of tongues

1 Corinthians 12:28

<u>He heals the brokenhearted and binds up their wounds</u>.

—Psalm 147:3

And the <u>prayer offered in faith will make the sick person well</u>; the Lord will raise him up. If he has sinned, he will be forgiven.

—James 5:15

And the Lord heard Hezekiah and <u>healed the people</u>.

—2 Chronicles 30:20

Large crowds followed him, and <u>he healed them there</u>.

—Matthew 19:2

The blind and the lame came to him at the temple, <u>and he healed them</u>.

—Matthew 21:14

Praise the Lord, O my soul, and forget not all his benefits—<u>who forgives all your sins and heals all your diseases, who redeems your life from the pit and</u>

<u>crowns you with love and compassion, who satisfies your desires with good things o that your youth is renewed like the eagle's.</u>

—Psalm 103:2-5

<u>Who had come to hear him and to be healed of their diseases? Those troubled by evil spirits were cured.</u>

—Luke 6:18

But the crowds learned about it and followed him. He welcomed them and spoke to them about the kingdom of God, and <u>healed those who needed healing</u>

—Luke 9:1

He sent forth his word and healed them; he rescued them from the grave.

—Psalm 107:20

Jesus said to him, "<u>I will go and heal him</u>."

—Matthew 8:7

📖 *They drove out many demons and anointed many sick people with oil and <u>healed them</u>.*

—Mark 6:13

📖 *But they remained silent. So taking hold of the man, <u>he healed him and sent him away</u>.*

—Luke 4:14

📖 *For the man who was <u>miraculously healed</u> was over forty years old.*

—Acts 4:22

📖 *The Spirit of the Sovereign Lord is on me, because the Lord has anointed me to preach good news to the poor. <u>He has sent me to bind up the brokenhearted, to proclaim freedom for the captives and release from darkness for the prisoners</u>*

—Isaiah 61:1

📖 *O Lord my God, <u>I called to you for help and you healed me</u>.*

—Psalms 30:2

So he replied to the messengers, "Go back and report to John what you have seen and heard: <u>The blind receive sight, the lame walk, those who have leprosy are cured, the deaf hear, the dead are raised, and the good news is preached to the poor.</u>"

—Luke 7:22

"I was enraged by his sinful greed; I punished him, and hid my face in anger, yet he kept on in his willful ways. I have seen his ways, <u>but I will heal him</u>; I will guide him and restore comfort to him, creating praise on the lips of the mourners in Israel. Peace, peace, to those far and near," says the Lord. "And I will heal them."

—Isaiah 57:18

Aware of this, Jesus withdrew from that place. <u>Many followed him, and he healed all their sick</u>.

—Matthew 12:15

<u>For he had healed many, so that those with diseases were pushing forward to touch him</u>.

—Mark 3:10

He could not do any miracles there, except <u>lay his hands on a few sick people and heal them. And he was amazed at their lack of faith</u>.

—Mark 6:5-6

Then Jesus said to the centurion, "Go! It will be done just <u>as you believed it would</u>." <u>And his servant was healed at that very hour.</u>

—Matthew 8:13

Jesus said to him, "Receive your sight; <u>your faith has healed you</u>."

—Luke 18:42

He said to her, <u>"Daughter, your faith has healed you.</u> Go in peace and be free from your suffering."

—Mark 5:34

Then Jesus answered, <u>"Woman, you have great faith! Your request is granted." And her daughter was healed from that very hour.</u>

—Matthew 15:28

Chapter 11

The Power of Words

For the kingdom of God is not a matter of talk but of power.

—1 Corinthians 4:20

Throughout the entire Bible, we are warned against false speech and the consequences it brings upon our physical and spiritual life. God has given us a mind to express our thoughts through the power of words.

But words are often misused, and this is one of the reason we fail in life. We were created to create a life desirable for us according to God's standards, to possess the power of "supernatural human beings." But for centuries the human population has lived in darkness in regards to how life is to be lived and understandably so. We have not created it, so how would we know how to live it without proper counsel from the creator of life?

However in order to live up to our intended purpose, it's important to understand that our words have power. We know this is true because words are an expression of our thoughts and those thoughts produce images in accordance with the nature of the thought, and in our mind, those images can cause positive or negative reactions in our bodies. A thought can make you laugh, cry, or sweat. It creates feelings of jealousy, anger, or rage. They are also responsible for our strength.

Our intimate desires are also triggered through our thoughts. Through these obvious facts, its clear to understand that everything in our physical nature (glands, muscles, blood, and organs), which is all there is, responds to our every thought. Since a thought has this much power, it should then be clear that that same power that's within the thought is within the word because the word is an expression of the thought. By this, our health, wealth, and position in life are established. We can never excel above what we think of ourselves and because our circumstances will always be a direct reflection of all we believe to be true.

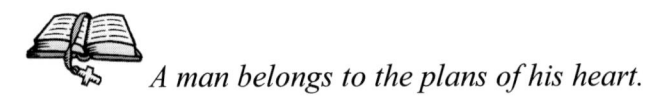

A man belongs to the plans of his heart.
—Proverbs 16:1

Since words are a product of thought, it creates in physical form the very nature of itself. Panic in the mind creates panic in the body.

This is the side of human life most people are unaware of. None of us dare to dream the impossible for fear of never achieving it. But scripture teaches us that "what's impossible for man is possible with God." We have the nature of God on the inside of us. Whatever our human nature cannot do, we can do through the spirit of God within us. The Bible teaches us that the kingdom of God lies within every human being and within this kingdom there's power. The Holy Spirit you accepted through Christ is your guide; its function is to develop your human spirit for spiritual power.

The world refuses the spirit of life because they would rather form all their opinions based on the visible world, not realizing that there is a spiritual world that governs this physical world.

During my personal quest for spiritual truth, I have come to understand that the words I used my entire life has been a direct reflection of the life I lived. But I wasn't overwhelmed by the conviction most people would feel when they are faced with the revelation that they may in fact be responsible for their life's order or, worse, that of their children's. Instead I rejoiced, for the answer for restoration was within the problem itself.

When that strong sense of conviction arrives accusing us of self-destruction, we are to accept it. That conviction signifies truth. The truth will always hurt, but it is when truth is present that change is able to take its stand. We all know that when sickness is present, it hurts, but it is with healing we are reformed with new life. Change must run its course, and it is usually at the brink of destruction.

There is a purpose for all creation. Through Christ we were given the authority to rule and have dominion, the ability to overcome Satan and his destruction through the power of right thought expressed through words.

Have you ever even once considered the intended purpose of your thoughts? Your thoughts were intended to serve you. To allow you to see things beyond their physical existence. To bring forth things you desire by faith, from the spiritual realm of life forces where all things begin, so that you will be justified through faith bringing glory to God. Christ demonstrated this being the power of God expressed on earth.

Our words establish our life just as God's words took form and created the universe. And if God spoke words to form the universe, they must hold power. And if we speak words to form our world, then wouldn't it be fair to say that we were given that same power? After all, he said we were made like him with this ability.

But if words meant nothing, then why did God create them and speak them? And how did all his words take form? Why do our words take form? Look at everything you have from your physical ailment to physical things. Do you not have evidence of the very words yourself have spoken? Although you may not have intentionally bought certain conditions and circumstances on yourself, but in hindsight, you did it all the same simply by believing in the possibility.

All of our words became a reality by faith in them. Now you may say, "Well, I don't have everything I said, because if that was the case, I should have much more than what I have now." But the reality is, you only have what you *believe* in your heart is possible for you, good or bad. Our belief that's rooted deep down within our heart is what grows into our lives.

As an example, if you say, "I have always wanted to be a millionaire". That cannot become a reality for you if you cannot believe you could physically obtain it, and the Bible refers to those kinds of words as idle, empty, with no feeling of faith behind them.

Now on the contrary, you may say, "Both my mother and father have diabetes, I already know I'm going to get it too." Because this is truth for you, it will become a fact in your life. You believe it because you are led by what's been planted on the inside of you and you see the curse operating with in your own family. Also you have been told about this possibility from your parents to your doctors from childhood till now. You have made this fact a reality long before it will show up in physical form. That's faith in fear. You have established it for yourself years ago through the power of your words by faith, so it must show up by spiritual law.

The Bible says, "Whatever you ask for believing that you have received it, you shall have it." Accepting something to be true for you is a form of asking by faith. Your human spirit only knows to grow what's been planted in the garden of your heart. The ground is no respecter of seed just as God is no respecter of person. He sends forth his rain on all, the good and the bad.

Words are of great value to mankind; God gave them to us to be like him in his likeness. Now in order to create a man in his likeness, we have to have the same ability and power in the spiritual realm since we have a spiritual blueprint.

> *Man is not to live on bread alone, but by every word that comes out of the mouth of God."*
>
> —Deuteronomy 8:3

> *The spirit gives life, the flesh counts for nothing. The words I have spoken to you are spirit, they are life. Yet there are some of you who do not believe.*
>
> —John 6:63-34

Words are like seeds. "You reap what you sow" applies to the words we use in addition to our actions. The Bible refers to our words as seeds and our heart (spirit) as the ground in which they will grow.

What you currently believe has been planted in your spirit by your words. The more you say something, the more you begin to believe it, the more it becomes a part of you. For this reason, compulsive liars will begin to believe their own lies.

Life should be a pleasure to live if we can begin to understand the power of the tongue. There are a multitude of scripture throughout the old and the New Testament confirming this fact.

Death and life are in the power of the tongue, and those who love it will eat its fruits.

—Proverbs 18:21

I encourage you to carefully read these scriptures below regarding words. They will open your eyes and give you insight and wisdom. There is no need for me to further explain this truth; the proof and power is within God's very own words.

Whoever would love life and see good days must keep his tongue from deceitful speech.

—1 Peter 3:10

He who guards his lips guards his life, but he who speaks rashly will come to ruin.

—Proverbs 13:3

The tongue also is a fire, a world of evil among the parts of the body. It corrupts the whole person, sets the whole course of his life on fire, and is itself set on fire by hell.

—James 3:16

Their throats are open graves; their tongues practice deceit. The poison of vipers is on their lips. Their mouths are full of cursing and bitterness. Their feet are swift to shed blood; ruin and misery mark their ways.

—Proverbs 3:13-16

For by your words you will be acquitted, and by your words you will be condemned.

—Matthew 12:37

An evil man is trapped by his sinful talk, but the righteous man escapes trouble.

—Proverbs 12:13

Jesus answered, "It is written: 'Man does not live on bread alone, but on every word that comes from the mouth of God.'"

—Matthew 4:4

My message and my preaching were not with wise and persuasive words, but with a demonstration of the Spirit's power.

—1 Corinthians 2:4

Wisdom will save you from the ways of wicked men, from men whose words are perverse.

—Proverbs 1:12

Pay attention to what I say; listen closely to my words. Do not let them out of your sight, keep them within your heart, for they are life to those who find them and health to a man's whole body.

—Proverbs 4:20-22

Blessings crown the head of the righteous, but violence overwhelms the mouth of the wicked.

—Proverbs 10:6

The wise in heart accept commands, but a chattering fool comes to ruin.

—Proverbs 10:8

He who winks maliciously causes grief, and a chattering fool comes to ruin.

—Proverbs 10:10

The mouth of the righteous is a fountain of life, but violence overwhelms the mouth of the wicked.

—Proverbs 10:11

Wise men store up knowledge, but the mouth of a fool invites ruin.

—Proverbs 10:13

He who conceals his hatred has lying lips and who ever spreads slander is a fool.

—Proverbs 10:18

When words are not many, sin is absent, but he who holds his tongue is wise.

—Proverbs 10:19

What the wicked dreads will overtake him; what the righteous desire will be granted.

—Proverbs 10:24

The mouth of the righteous brings forth wisdom, but a perverse tongue will be cut out.

—Proverbs 10:31

The lips of the righteous know what is fitting, but the mouth of the wicked only what is perverse.

—Proverbs 10:32

With his mouth the godless destroys his neighbor, but through knowledge the righteous escape.

—Proverbs 11:9

> *Through the blessing of the upright a city is exalted, but by the mouth of the wicked it is destroyed.*
>
> —Proverbs 11:11

> *A man who lacks judgment derides his neighbor, but a man of understanding holds his tongue.*
>
> —Proverbs 11:12

> *The words of the wicked lie in wait for blood, but the speech of the upright rescues them.*
>
> —Proverbs 12:6

> *A man is praised according to his wisdom, but men with warped minds are despised.*
>
> —Proverbs 12:8

> *From the fruit of his lips a man is filled with good things as surely as the work of his hands rewards.*
>
> —Proverbs 12:14

Reckless words pierce like a sword, but the tongue of the wise brings healing.

—Proverbs 12:18

Truthful lips endure forever, but a lying tongue lasts only a moment.

—Proverbs 12:19

From the fruit of his lips a man enjoys good things, but the unfaithful have a craving for violence.

—Proverbs 13:2

She speaks with wisdom, and faithful instruction is on her tongue.

—Proverbs 21:36

The good man brings good things out of the good stored up in his heart, and the evil man brings evil things out of the evil stored up in his heart. For out of the overflow of his heart his mouth speaks.

—Luke 6:45

📖 *The spirit gives life; the flesh counts for nothing. The words I have spoken to you are spirit and they are life.*

—John 6:6

📖 *Do not let any unwholesome talk come out of your mouths, but only what is helpful for building others up according to their needs, that it may benefit those who listen.*

—Ephesians 4:29

📖 *But I tell you that men will have to give account on the Day of Judgment for every careless word they have spoken.*

—Matthew 12:36

📖 *For by your words you will be acquitted, and by your words you will be condemned.* [Words have the power to save or destroy you.]

—Matthew 12:37

Make a tree good and its fruit will be good, or make a tree bad and its fruit will be bad, for a tree is recognized by its fruit. You brood of vipers, how can you who are evil say anything good? For out of the overflow of the heart the mouth speaks.

—Matthew 12:33-35

What goes into a man's mouth does not make him "unclean," but what comes out of his mouth, that is what makes him "unclean."

—Matthew 15:11

For it is with your heart that you believe and are justified, and it is with your mouth that you confess and are saved.

—Romans 10:10

Would he argue with useless words, with speeches that have no value?

—Job 15:3

Let your conversation be always full of grace, seasoned with salt, so that you may know how to answer everyone.

—Colossians 4:6

But just as you excel in everything—in faith, in speech, in knowledge, in complete earnestness and in your love for us—see that you also excel in this grace of giving.

—2 Corinthians 8:7

For in him you have been enriched in every way—in all your speaking and in all your knowledge.

—1 Corinthians 1:5

Chapter 12

The Heart of Life

We look to medical science for cures in hopes to be delivered from some deadly disease, but they fail us every time. But this shouldn't be a surprise to those who are in Christ because man is not the creator of life, so how could they promise it in any measure. Let us first establish the fact that our Creator has created and given us everything we need to preserve life.

> *His divine power has given us everything we need for life and godliness through our knowledge of him who called us by his own glory and goodness.*
>
> —2 Peter 1:3

Anything synthetic given to us as a remedy for health or healing serves only as temporary counterfeit to the real thing; therefore, they can only provide a temporary fix. For this reason, healing cannot be assured. Since true health begins with faith in our spirits ability of restoration, God has provided medical and natural provisions to act only as an *aid* to our spirit in the process of restoration not because he felt as if his healing power wasn't enough but because of our rebellious nature, our pride and ignorance in regards tp the source of health.

Sure, God has provided us with natural health-retaining substances found in vegetation along with the hidden life-saving treasures of our ecosystems, but even those substances serve as a temporary fix because they are all created things and are, therefore, subject to destruction.

The source of health and vitality begins in the human spirit, through knowledge of who God has created you to be. Our bodies are just an expression of that spirit. Anything synthetic in actuality is designed to work in opposition to the law of life because it was created apart from all the essentials that created life; therefore, it can never have a permanent role in it.

It's never wise to rely totally on doctors or medicine as the source of health, but to view them as only an aid to the spirit of life will be more beneficial in your recovery process because by doing so, you are acknowledging your life-sustaining source as the creator and maintainer of life. Although God has equipped them with the knowledge and ability to provide a much needed service, they should never be viewed as our source of health and vitality. If we should find ourselves in need of any kind of medical treatment, whether it be some synthetic regimen or surgery, we ought to pray in favor of God's supernatural healing ability working through the physician for our benefit.

Know that God has created natural resources as a temporary benefit to our health. Modern medicine can prove to be a faithful regimen to our ailment but only for a time by the power of hope and faith in it. Faith will work for anyone who puts it to practice in any area of life, but whether healing is there to stay will be dependent upon the source in which one has planted his or her faith. If that faith is in synthetic resources, although the appearance of life may be present at the time, when the FDA recalls that drug or notifies the public of the newfound dangers of that drug, your faith will die along with the drug, and if you have given your life over to the the drug of which you feel is the source of your recovery, then so will you.

On the other hand, if that faith is planted in the healing power of God working on the inside of you, true health is summoned and is therefore established through his power and it shall remain.

Natural and synthetic resources do have some value but only as an aid to assist the human spirit in maintaining life.

Have nothing to do with godless myths and old wives' tales; rather, <u>train yourself to be godly</u>. For physical training is of some value, but godliness has value for all things, holding promise for both the present life and the life to come. This is a trustworthy saying that deserves full acceptance (and for this we labor and strive), that we have put our hope in the living God, who is the Savior of all men and especially of those who believe.

—1 Timothy 4:7-10

Chapter 13

God's Will Be Done

Those who are stricken with some sort of life-threatening disease often find themselves submitting to this deadly end, concluding that it must be God's will for their life. This way of thinking is usually stemmed from the end result of so many good God-fearing people who are good to all and loved by all but died an unnatural death nonetheless.

Also, they look back on their own life considering all the good they have done, the friends they have gained, and the people they have loved, never forming a solid conclusion as to why this has happened to them or their loved ones.

For this reason, they accept it as being their destiny. They become convinced within themselves that their pain and suffering is for the good of others or that someone must die in order for someone else to live. With this conclusion, they decide to fight what they call the good fight of faith by entering into a painful place of contentment in acceptance of their life-threatening inheritance. To give in to such a hopeless end is not a faith-building process but a dream killer.

I cannot stress enough the importance of faith. Failure is a form of death orchestrated by Satan, summoned through unbelief.

> *By faith in the name of Jesus, this man whom you see and know was made strong. It is Jesus' name and the faith that comes through him that has given this complete healing to him, as you can all see.*
>
> —Acts 3:16

> *Then Jesus said to the centurion, "Go! It will be done just as you believed it would." And his servant was healed at that very hour.*
>
> —Matthew 8:13

> *Jesus said to him, "Receive your sight; your faith has healed you."*
>
> —Luke 18:42

These holy scriptures are an expression of the importance and power of faith and how it works.

> *Without faith it is impossible to please God because anyone who comes to him must <u>believe</u> that he exists and that <u>he rewards those who eagerly seek him.</u>*
> —Hebrews 11:6

This promise of reward is not just one of heavenly value but of natural value as well. To know the power of God is to understand the purpose of salvation that came through Christ. To understand his ways is to be knowledgeable of the promises and provisions he provided through his covenant. To have faith in God is to be fully persuaded of his love for you by accepting the grace that was given as a free gift. To understand the love of God is to understand that he loves you in spite of who you are, not because of who you are.

There are spiritual promises regarding heaven, and then, there are natural promises regarding life on earth. The person that accepts unnatural death, discord, or affliction to be their destiny is unconsciously wicked. The Bible describes a wicked person as one who separates themselves from him by rejecting his his words.

Deuteronomy 28:20-22 teaches us that disease, unnatural death, poverty, and discord is a *curse for the wicked* while verses 1-14 expresses the blessings of obedience to his words, which is health, wealth, and peace.

This truth is not only documented throughout the Old Testament but was verified through the gospel of peace and reconciliation. It's imperative to understand that any kind of physical discomfort is a curse and were warranted for sinners throughout the entire Bible.

But since we are born into sin afforded by the rebellion of Adam, God in his loving mercy, summoned the repercussions of sin which were intended to turn the sinner from their sins, that we may enjoy this present life for the little time that we have on this earth. In our day, we have Christ as our Savior who delivers us from the destruction of this world, who redeemed from the curse that brought spiritual death, but because sin will remain in this physical world, we are still held captive by its conditions simply by participating in the sinful ways of the world. therefore, premature death through sickness and disease becomes inevitable. But those who are in Christ should know the deliverance that has been provided through the power of God, and in him, we should no longer accept its conditions.

Scripture teaches us all undesired conditions are the result of sin. Since the fall of man back in the Garden of Eden, sin possessed our minds, causing every man on earth to be born to sin. Now you may be saying, "So there you have it, we are all sinners no matter what, which means my ailment is justified." But you're wrong, *dead* wrong.

> *Jesus came to be a living sacrifice for our sins. He was pierced through for our transgression and was crushed for our iniquities. The <u>punishment that brought us peace</u> was upon him and <u>by his wounds we are healed.</u>*
>
> —Isaiah 53:5

> *He himself bore our sins in his body on the tree, so that we might die to sins and live for righteousness; by his wounds you have been healed.*
>
> —1 Peter 2:24

To live in peace means to live a life worth living with nothing to hinder us from growing into a complete expression of God. If such morbid conditions were his will, then life would be meaningless.

Yes, Jesus came as a spiritual guide for our souls, but he also came to give us peace here on earth; for this reason, he formed a healing ministry and healed people wherever he went, near and far, regardless of their sin, and he empowered his disciples to do the same. Never once did he justify disease, discord, or poverty for any man even though we were all wicked in our ways. His purpose was to demonstrate God's gifts of mercy and grace and his will for our lives, which were obviously for us to be comforted and delivered in our time of affliction.

Christ was knowledgeable of the sinful nature of a man's mind and the affliction it would impose on the human nature. But since he is our Savior, through the renewal of our minds, we no longer have to live according to the condition of our sinful nature. Through his blood we have been given wisdom, righteousness, sanctification, and redemption.

With all that and more to be said, we ourselves have to face some horrific facts and accept them as truth if we could ever hope to know the peace God has sent us by his grace. In this we should know that conviction causes change, growth, and healing. But what is the truth? Some may ask, "If this is not God's will then why am I sick?" The answer is simple but hard to accept. For those who are separated from a life in Christ is considered spiritually dead, and this spiritual death is a separation from God and his provisions. If we are separated from God, then we have no savior to deliver us from our troubles.

But let's also take note of the fact that there are many Christians who are experiencing a separation. These are the Christians who have accepted Christ as their Savior but have rejected the healing power of the Holy Spirit through their unbelief. They have plenty of head knowledge in regards to the grace of the almighty God and his healing powers, but they have not planted this knowledge in their hearts. They leave everything up to God, not acting on a single promise. But faith without deeds is dead.

Your words and acts express your faith in the promises of God, and by this, you establish them to be true for you. But if you claim to know the power of God but remain content with the death sentence that's been given to you, then you have not understood the ministry of Jesus as it should be nor have you accepted his purpose to benefit your life now. Those who have no true knowledge of God are blinded by Satan's schemes in regard to the promises and provisions for their life now, and because of these things, they have accepted what Satan has suggested pertaining to their life just as Adam and Eve did regarding their life. They answered God with Satan's testimony.

God asked Adam, "Why are you hiding?" Adam answered, "I am naked." God replied, "Who told you were naked?"

God was fully aware of whom Adam was listening to and the condition of his mind and knew that they were under the influence of Satan. Both Adam and Eve believed Satan's word above God's word, and since the wages of sin is death, through their sin, death for all living things has entered the earth.

Sickness finds its origin in fear, and Satan is the god of fear. By accepting those conditions, you too are answering God with Satan's testimony.

God will say, "Where have you been?" You said, "Dying from cancer." God said, "Who told you that you were going to die from cancer?"

This is what God has to say regarding your misfortune.

Did I not say that you are an over comer by the word of your testimony? Did I not say that you are more than a conqueror? Romans 8:37 Did I not tell you to "be strong in me and in my mighty power and to put on my full armor, so that you can stand against *the devils schemes. I told you that your struggles is not against your flesh and blood but against the rulers, against the authorities and against the powers of this dark world and against the spiritual forces of evil in the heavenly realms. For this reason I advised you to put on the full armor of God, so that when the day of evil comes, you may be able to stand your ground, and to stand firm with the belt of truth buckled around your waist, with the breast plate of righteousness in place and to have your feet fitted <u>with the readiness that comes from the gospel of peace.</u> In addition to this, I fully advised you to . . . ." Take up the shield of faith, with which you can extinguish all the flaming arrows of the evil one and to take up the helmet of salvation and the sword of the spirit, which is the word of God.*

—Ephesians 6:10-17

For I am the God who have created you in my image and likeness with powers to cast down spiritual wickedness. Because you have given in to the devils schemes, you have rendered my word ineffective against you and brought this calamity to yourself.

—Romans 2:8-9

When you accepted my dear son as Lord and high priest, you were delivered from the power of darkness and translated into his kingdom.

—Colossians 1:13

I have given you authority to use my name.

—John 16:23

I have given you my divine powers and everything you need for life and godliness through your knowledge of me. Through these I have given you very great and precious promises so that thorough them you may participate in my divine nature and escape the corruption in the world caused by evil desires.

—2 Peter 1:3-4

I told you to trust in me and lean not unto your own understanding.

—Proverbs 3:5

📖 *I told you to acknowledge me in all your ways so that I may direct your path.*

—Proverbs 3:6

📖 *I promised you that I will perfect that which concerns you.*

—Psalms 138:8

📖 *That I will command my angels concerning you to guard you in all your ways, that they will lift you up in their hands so that you will not strike your foot against a stone... I said that you will tread upon the lion and the serpent and if you love me, I will rescue you. I promised to protect you who acknowledge my name, and that you can call upon me and I will answer you. I promised to be with you in trouble, I promised to deliver you and honor you. With long life, I promised to satisfy you and show you my "salvation."*

—Psalms 91:11-16

Those who believe that disease and unnatural death, poverty or discord of any kind are God's will for the redeemed will find that there is no corresponding scripture to confirm this false belief except through unbelief. However, it does mention long-suffering, perseverance, and hope for his people.

> *Not only so, but we also rejoice in our sufferings, because we know that suffering produces perseverance; perseverance, character; and character, hope. <u>And hope does not disappoint us,</u> because God has poured out his love into our hearts by the Holy Spirit, whom he has given us.*
> —Romans 5:3-5

Hope does not disappoint us. We will get what we hold on to. Perseverance does not mean to accept our circumstances, but to stand on God's promise regardless of what our present circumstances offer and to wait for what has been promised. It means to know his will and to stay the same in faith no matter what.

If God wanted us to accept the destruction that accompanies our ailments, then he wouldn't have given us the provisions to fight it. If he is the one who created it, then he wouldn't have provided the means and the power of faith to fight it; it would make sense to just eliminate all the natural resources he provided from our lives.

Satan is the ruler of darkness. In his hands is the power of evil, fear, and suggestion; that's all he has, and his suggestion involves personal influences in hopes to convince us that pain and suffering is our lot in life and we should just accept such circumstances.

This false sense of contentment keeps us rooted and established in fear because it goes against the living word of God.

Satan is the father of lies. Anything that will hinder us from completing God's given assignment in this life or living a life worth living is the manipulation of the devil.

How can we help the sick, feed the hungry, raise our children, manage our affairs if we ourselves stand defeated. In this state of mind, our purpose on earth would be useless; it would have been better if we were never born. If there is no purpose to serve, life would be meaningless. For God to separate his children by afflicting deadly disasters upon some and peace upon others is unfair.

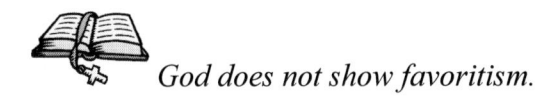

God does not show favoritism.

—Romans 2:11

In this state of mind, we are no earthly good to mankind so why bother showing up for life? It will be better for us to just give up living altogether and allow our bodies the death it deserves, if we are to believe that all of our rewards are in heaven alone.

As for me, I will take all the earthy blessings that God has in store for me now that I might live life in the full measure of it, being able to bless others along the way. We were not created to suffer, but to overcome all adversities through his power that is at work within us.

This does not mean that we will live life in a breeze. Satan will always challenge our physical nature in attempts to lay his foundation of conflict, but our job is to never negotiate with him. Our job is to get acquainted with the promises of God and use the authority we have in Christ by speaking faith-filled words over our circumstances.

A thousand may fall at your side, ten thousand at your right hand, but it will not come near you.
—Psalm 91:7

I strongly urge all readers of this book to observe the verses below that you might become fully persuaded of God's promises concerning our life.

Chapter 14

The Spirit's Call

A man's spirit sustains him in sickness, but a crushed spirit who can bear?

—Proverbs 18:14

Damage done to your mind is damage done to your body. Unhealthy thought patterns are one of the primary causes for discomfort and disease. The spirit within is the life behind every function of the human body and is responsible for where you are today. And it has a way of warning us when a bad thought is received. So when we think about the worst thing that can possibly happen to us or a loved one in a traumatic situation and we feel a sense of uneasiness associated with that thought, know that it's your spirit disagreeing with your current thoughts. In truth, it is urging us to change our thinking by being positive or else. Most of us ignore this uneasiness; by doing so we feed the potential disaster and bring it to life.

Your spirit functions according to the kingdom of God. It's there for you to benefit from it. Even unbelievers who believe everything just happens, finds him or herself praying for a good result in time of desperation, and when all turns out well, they fail to realize that it was the power of God, the strength of the spirit within them, that gave them the cause (*silent prayer*), to get the effect (*results desired*). So their disclaimer is "I stopped my panic because I had a feeling it would be okay."

> *My grace is sufficient for you, for my power is made perfect in your weakness.*
>
> —2 Corinthians 12:9

We were given the power through our spirit to conquer all things spiritual based in fear and anxiety through faith. That's the reason we find power in times of need and strength after an illness has left our bodies. That is our spirit operating to perfection.

By acknowledging the spirit within and its purpose of growth and restoration, we can regain control of our lives by creating the proper environment within our minds, which in turn will allow our spirit to run free to thrive and produce according to its nature. We must allow it to be the pilot of our lives by listening to the warning signs when we are in bad spirits. As an example, many of us when we are in strife with another person and become resentful and unforgiving, although we feel justified by the wrong done to us, we also feel a sense of wrongdoing. We know deep down inside that we should forgive and let it go, and so we say, "I know it's wrong to hold a grudge and I should forgive them, but . . ."

Every time you feel discomfort in any way, shape, or form, take heed, knowing that it is your spirit urging you to change the direction of your thoughts, or else you will suffer the consequences.

> Do not be deceived: God cannot be mocked. A man reaps what he sows. *The one who sows to please his sinful nature, from that nature will reap destruction; the one who sows to please the Spirit, from the Spirit will reap eternal life.*
> —Galatians 6:7-8

In most cases, we have all felt a sense of uncertainty or uneasiness at the start of the thought. But then our sinful nature takes over and begins to suggest that we pursue it in fear. The sinful nature, our bodies, is always in need of instant gratification of some kind whether it be food, sex, drugs, or anger; it doesn't matter. It wants what it wants and it wants it now, so it tells us to ignore the hunch and go after the goods, and Satan is there to confirm the illusion with the promise of destruction as an end result. In all cases, our confession at the end of any wrong doing or wrong response will always be "I should've listened to my instinct."

Know that your body is your worst enemy. It screams out for attention, and because we have given into it for so long, it will be a painful process in restoring it to back to its natural state but not impossible. We can overcome our flesh by simply not giving in to it. We often try to enforce this same principle in the lives of our children and loved ones. We deny them the things we know will harm them no matter how loud their little souls scream for it. By this simple process of elimination, healthy habits are formed within our children. The power that feeds their sinful nature lies within our hands, and we fight it every day through discipline. They have no choice but to surrender their will and persevere through the storm. But we, as adults, find it hard to follow the very principle we ourselves enforce. We then become guilty in the eyes of God.

You hypocrite, first take the plank out of your own eye, and then you will see clearly to remove the speck from your brother's eye.

—Matthew 7:5

We cannot love others more than we love ourselves. We are to do unto others as we would have them do unto us. We must be willing to make the same sacrifices we insist on. The way that's most beneficial in teaching our children to live by the spirit and to deny the flesh is to openly demonstrate this principle operating in our own lives in view of our children. This goes for every area of life. If we are to instill moral values within our children, we must first understand for ourselves our Creator's divine purpose of marriage, teach it to our children, and then become a living example of sexual morality by not engaging ourselves in relationships outside of marriage, and the same principle applies to everything we do. God would never ask you to follow a command in your own strength and neither should we enforce this requirement upon another person. We have the Holy Spirit as our guide. We can become sensitive to his voice by acknowledging his presence. His promises are food for the soul. They are filled with wisdom and insight, and our spirit grows and develops from them.

Therefore, rid yourselves of all malice and all deceit, hypocrisy, envy, and slander of every kind. Like newborn babies, crave pure spiritual milk, so that by it you may grow up in your salvation, now that you have tasted that the Lord is good.

—1 Peter 2:1

Do not submit yourselves to the rules of this world; do not be led by your physical senses but be led by the spirit and the power of God.

Living abundantly above sickness and poverty is our blood-bought right. It has already been established in heaven that we are heirs to God's kingdom that dwells within the very heart of us. We have also been given authority and dominion to rule over all things of this earth. We are the children of the most high God, the creator and owner of all things in the heavens and on the earth, and as heirs, we have a right to all things through the blood of Jesus.

But those who are spiritually discerned will never know the benefits of being led by the spirit. They will spend their lives trying to obtain wealth, health, and peace by physical means and labor based on what they see by attempting to change what's already a physical fact instead of changing the spiritual reality from which all things are brought forth through the power of one's own mind.

Having wisdom of the spirit is to be able to discern spiritual realities from physical facts. Being spiritually enlightened is a spiritual gift from God; a trust entrusted to you that enables you to see what the naked eye cannot.

An eye that is naked is an eye that is enabled to see the physical things of the world, objects, traffic, people, environment, but is unable to see the *cause behind* the effects because the cause is hidden from it. Cause is a spiritual law that governed the physical effects of all things seen. So their life becomes governed by their senses, what they see, feel, taste, smell, and hear, limiting their ability to live up to their true potential. And did I mention that these people fall under a curse?

> *Hear this, you foolish and senseless people, who have eyes but do not see, who have ears but do not hear.*
> —Jeremiah 5:21

> *Son of man, you are living among a rebellious people. They have eyes to see but do not see and ears to hear but do not hear, for they are a rebellious people.*
> —Ezekiel 12:2

But the spiritual eye hides itself behind the physical eye. It's our state of consciousness which enables us to enter therein having disabled the physical eye itself. Anyone may enter into this secret wisdom; the only requirement is that he closes his eyes to the world so that his mind can be opened to the things of God.

> *Do not conform any longer to the pattern of this world, but be transformed by the renewing of your mind. Then you will be able to test and approve what God's will is—his good, pleasing and perfect will.*
>
> —Romans 12:2

> *But blessed are your eyes because they see, and your ears because they hear. For I tell you the truth, many prophets and righteous men longed to see what you see but did not see it, and to hear what you hear but did not hear it.*
>
> —Matthew 13:16-17

It can see beyond the problem and knows that within the problem lies the solution. The spiritual eye can take the bad conditions in which he is living and turn it around for the good, in doing so, he releases the power to change its effects by changing the cause which intimately lies within himself. The spiritual eye surrenders to truth no matter how hurtful and self-convicting that truth may be but at the same time rejoices for having found the truth and the answer to all his problems. It brings light on any situation one might find himself in and his secret wisdom discovers the *self-altering* solution, which will eventually free him from the thing that holds him captive.

We live in two realms of life, one temporal and the other everlasting.

Our spiritual eyes, which are usually referred to as *the third eye*, is far more powerful than the natural eye. It gives us peace about a thing; it guides us in our decision making and senses danger from another as well as reveals things that are hidden from the natural eye.

But when the two are working together, the third eye looks to the imagination for its desires and the physical eye corresponds with the object seen in the mind. All things seen and desired becomes a living reality, and the Holy Spirit becomes your guide in life that brings us in harmony with our greatest and highest good as a direct result of our inner state of mind.

> *Are you so foolish? After <u>beginning with the Spirit</u>, are you now trying to attain your goal by human effort?*
>
> —Ephesians 3:3

The Bible says that the Holy Spirit will lead and guide us into all that is true. His mission is to cleanse us of all unrighteousness and bring us to the place where God has ordained for us while we were still in our mothers' wombs. It's a place of total life prosperity, lacking nothing in every area of life, to take ownership of the blessing, which is part of our inheritance during our stay on earth, and to be anointed with spiritual power to make a difference to the human race. All that God wants us to receive is governed and administered through the law of faith and faith works by love. These two things are vital to our success and purpose. We cannot have one without the other.

Though the pathway seems simple, the gate remains narrow. Only a few will get in because they are willing to trade their thoughts for the thoughts of God, their visions for God's vision, and their reasonings for God's wisdom. Very few are willing to drop their garment of sin, even after they have learned it's the primary cause of their destruction.

But when a person is willing to live by faith and walk in love at any cost, all that is good becomes their own, so fear of not having can never contaminate your rightly ordered thought. Because they now understand the hidden dangers that fear, hatred, envy, strife, jealousy, unforgiveness, drunkenness, lying, impurity, gossip, slander, fornication, and adultery amongst many others, have led them into destruction, they keep these things far from them.

The road is a hard and tedious one; a mountain that starts out wide with many hungry for the promise of peace. But as you travel along the path of righteousness with your eyes closed to the world, you wake up halfway up only to find that those who were with you have fallen and given up the journey and you are now alone. You have substituted pleasure for pain. You have chosen to be naked by having exposed of all evil schemes hidden within your heart as one goes before a court and confesses all the laws he has broken, therefore subjecting himself to punishment or death.

You have nowhere to hide and no net in which to catch your fall. You have given up self-preservation and took up the shield of faith as your safety net and your anchor. You have allowed your mind to become one with God and what was once enjoyable to you becomes a nightmare in which you have awakened from.

Having closed your eyes to the world around you, you now have no visual influences to seduce you into deliberate sin. The sinful city is at your feet, and it is still a struggle having given up the people you thought were good for you; sorrow now takes its toll on your emotions. You want to go back, but enlightened with the truth, it now becomes impossible due to the strong conviction that is now present with the thought. You become trapped by what you know, and the term *ignorance is bliss* has a purposeful meaning. Peace becomes your aim, and you must travel thereof.

Though broken, exposed, dirty, beaten, bruised, and helpless in your own strength, you are unwilling to fall back into the hell of which you climbed out of.

At this point in time, you will begin to look to God for his strength and mercy, and it is at this point on the mountain that he meets you where you are at your worst as you screamed his name in the depths of your heart and even made an idle threat, a demand for him to save you or else. He responds to the blood-wrenching cry that stood at the door of your lips. He begins to heal the wounds that occurred along your journey. By this you surrender all you have for all that he has.

It is at this place you are delivered. This place on the mountain becomes your home for a while until you are strong enough to proceed along the path of righteousness. The fruits of righteousness begin to develop within you, and joy now takes the place of sadness. Peace in the place of affliction. Love in the place where hate once brooded. Forgiveness in the place of resentment. Good thoughts in the place of bad ones, and good words in the place of bad words.

You have let God's light direct your path, and now you are transformed and renewed like an eagle.

Therefore, if anyone is in Christ, he is a new creation; the old has gone, the new has come!
—2 Corinthians 5:17

As an eagle is the strongest predator of the air, it loses all seven thousand feathers, its beak, along with its strength, and searches to find shelter for which he can hide in order for his wounds to heal, his feathers to be restored, and its beak renewed. In the same way, so must we.

As an eagle, we become victorious more than conquerors.

He humbled you causing you to hunger and then fed you with manna, which neither you nor your fathers had known, to teach you that man does not live on bread alone but on every word that comes from the mouth of God.
—Deuteronomy 8:3

Chapter 15

The Power of Forgiveness

And when you stand praying, if you hold anything against anyone, forgive him, so that you're Father in heaven may forgive you your sins.

—Mark 11:25

This is one of my favorite scriptures. Its a clear representation of love, unity and humility. It teaches us that for one; we are to love one another which is the second highest commandment in light of the first which is to love God first. A person who is able to love God who he cannot see first will then be able to love the one he can see. It also teaches us the importance of others in our lives and in the world itself as a whole, unity. That there are people in this world that we would consider beneath us, a drunkard, a addict, a murderer or a prostitute. Let us first establish the fact that we are all sinners. The only thing that separates one sin from another is the level of harm involved. Therefore, we should never pass judgement in regards to a persons salvation based on what he has done because we have all fallen short of God's perfect standard of holiness and the bible clearly teaches us that if we have broken one commandment we have broken them all. In this rule the liar or the thief is as guilty as the murderer and is under the same judgement. This brings us full circle back to the first and second commandment. Love your neighbor as you would love yourself. We are all in need of God's grace when it comes to salvation and even more so when it comes down to the satanic spirit that is so prevalent with the human soul. Its in tended purpose is to corrupt the human soul and so it finds the weaker and most vulnerable vessel as its host to express his destruction to the world. Now although it may be true that sin has its repercussions here on this earth but at the same time Christ came and offered himself as a living sacrifice to redeem us from the eternal destruction that our sins deserved. His blood reconciled us back into a relationship with our heavenly father and because of the payment he made, the sins of all man has been forgiven.

When you were dead in your sins and in the uncircumcision of your sinful nature, God mad;e you alive with Christ. He forgave us all our sins, having cancelled the written code with its regulations that was against us and that stood opposed to us; he took it away, nailing it to the cross.

-Colossians 2: 13-14

By this act of grace-we humble ourselves in the presence of God knowing that our goodness is not the source of our salvation. Therefore, we identify ourselves with those whom we consider to be sinful, placing ourselves on equal ground so that through it, compassion can take root. Forgiveness is the ripened fruit of compassion.

But before we can begin to truly forgive someone without any strings or stipulations, we must first bring ourselves to a complete understanding as to why God insist on it. What value and impact does it have on our lives here.

The act of forgiveness can be a hard and difficult thing for many people to accept who are unaware of the biblical truth and the spiritual benefit behind it. Whether it is to be given or received, the lack of it has become a stumbling block for many of us and has secretly hindered our growth within our spirit as well as our bodies. Unforgiveness is an unfruitful seed that once it is established through offense, grows into strife, resentment, anger, bitterness, and rage. As i have demonstrated in the previous chapters, when those emotions are present within a person's mind, the side effects take place in the body, causing a hazardous environment. It throws all the functions of the human body off course as hatred lays its foundation within the human soul.

Anyone who believes that forgiveness should be earned or withheld due to a suffered wrong will not only continue to live a chaotic life afforded by the evil he or she carry in their heart, but will also find that their environment and social circle are a direct reflection of all that they they are, if they are willing to look closely at their thoughts.

When we pray to our Lord about our problems, we are seeking deliverance in those areas. As God sends his deliverance through the hands of other people, the unforgiveness you hold in your heart becomes a blessing blocker; consequently, the very thing that threatens your well-being becomes your destruction. It has found a familiar host in which to dwell.

Whatever good we want to manifest in our life is automatically, by law, taken down or cancelled out by the evil thoughts of one's mind toward another. This is because evil thoughts are accompanied by stronger emotions and becomes the predominate thought, and by the law of return, we attract back to us what we send out in thought toward another.

When we become hurt or offended by someone, we become resentful. We talk about it and wear this open scar on our sleeve for everyone to see and to come into agreement with our offense as we begin putting up boundaries for everyone. But in this state of thought, we then expect the worst out of most people and circumstances. This is all done out of fear of being hurt again.

Every setback in life becomes confirmation of our past disappointments, and in our minds, our actions of unforgiveness becomes justified. The people we have forgiven in the past are put back in a box, shipped off with the current offenders, and accusation waits at the door of our lips. But to slander another person, a child of God, is the same as slandering God since his spirit dwells within the very heart of that person, although unapparent. Every action or word of any kind operates in the law of return therefore, to curse his creation is to summon a curse upon ourselves.

To live with unforgiveness is to feel a sense of abuse, and in the secret places of the mind, one would begin to wish harm on the offender becoming fully persuaded that they deserve every evil thing that comes their way. But what people have failed to realize is that the seeds we plant in the garden of life will be the harvest in which we will ultimately reap. Its just a matter of time.

Do not be deceived, God cannot be mocked. A man reaps what he sows.

—Galatians 6:7

The reason God set the commandment of *love* as being the greatest commandment above all is because we are all one with God and his spirit dwells in us all as one single spirit. So when we make a choice to curse another human being, we reject his spirit working within that person, and by the law of return, we subconsciously reject that very same spirit working within ourselves, and by this we separate ourselves from God and his abundant provisions of grace. As children of God, we should never intentionally cause harm to any human soul and we expect the same in return. But the reality is that we are all born into a broken world made imperfect by sin; therefore, we are not currently saved from it. When a person becomes saved, a spiritual process of restoration takes place within the human soul. Sins are dealt with silently, individually. The stronger the habit, the harder it will be to break, so it will take some time. But understand that it can be a slow process depending on a person's ability or willingness to change; therefore change is not always immediate, and it is because of this silent process, a saved person does not appear to be saved. The person will look and act the same coming out as they did going in.

Understand this one thing: if we had the ability or power to transform ourselves in our own strength, we would all choose to live up to life's highest form, pure love, strong faith, compassion, joy, meekness, patience, kindness, and humility. Unfortunately, that's an unrealistic expectation for any of us to dream. The only one who has mastered that is Christ himself. If God required that of us, we would all fall short.

Because we are unable to change ourselves, it would be an unfair requirement of someone else. We all need help at being our best, and with the help of the Holy Spirit, we can overcome any strong hold. It's the Holy Spirit's job to filter out the wheat from the tares, so to speak. But this spiritual process cannot take place until the saved person surrenders their will, their way.

We are all connected through Christ Jesus. The patience he has extended toward you in your rebellion is extended by grace to everyone.

The Bible teaches us that Christ is the head of us all and that we are all the body of Christ. With this insight, as a unit, one body part should not antagonize, criticize, or curse the other.

The body is a unit, though it is made of many parts; and though all its parts are many, they form one body. So it is with Christ. For we are all baptized by one Spirit into one body—whether Jews or Greek, slave or free—and we were all given the one Spirit to drink.

—1 Corinthians 12:12-13

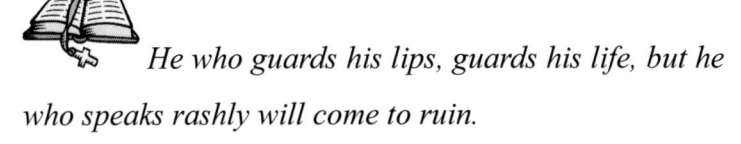

He who guards his lips, guards his life, but he who speaks rashly will come to ruin.

—Proverbs 13:3

Far too often we let our feelings govern our lives. Most people are ignorant to the fact that forgiveness is a gift from God. He gives it to us freely, without judgment, in spite of who we are so that with the same spirit of love, we can also give it freely without judgment or condition. If we had to pay for our sins in sweat, blood, and tears in order to earn God's forgiveness, we would never have it; in fact, we would be automatically doomed to eternal destruction. Therefore, to make someone pay for something God has given you freely is not only selling something that's not for sale but also ultimately putting a price tag on something that belongs to God. It was never ours to sell to begin with.

We expect God to overlook and forgive our transgressions, our shortcomings, our temperament, and he does. But not when you call on him but before. He has already made the provision for it through the blood of the Christ. You see, Christ took care of our sins before we were ever born, so forgiveness cannot be based on what we can do to earn it but on what Christ has done in order for us to receive it by God's grace. So when we choose to sell the very thing God has given us as a free gift, we rebel against his designed purpose of forgiveness, which will ultimately separate us from his divine goodness.

Most people rather not forgive, believing the other person will feel as if they have won or gotten over on them, that if we give them this without any consequences, they will only repeat the offense, so *we* should be the one to show them how wrong they are by withholding our love, or they will claim to have forgiven them but, in action, choose to hold on to the offense against them. That's not forgiving. That's waiting for another offense to add to the current offense. By this act, you are in actuality only hurting yourself because you're the only one who will suffer from it.

To forgive is to completely let go of an offense, not allowing that offense to hinder the good God wants you to extend toward that person or another. I'm not suggesting that one should become a doormat for the offender, but if we can learn to deal with them according to their spiritual immaturity, which is clearly demonstrated through their actions, and with opened eyes in regards to the infallible law of return, we would find the compassion needed in order to forgive them based on the irreversible harm that they have summonsed to themselves.

Unforgiveness also works against our physical nature. Each unhealthy thought you have will have a negative effect on your body due to the strong negative emotions that accompany it.

> *Let no debt remain outstanding, except the continuing debt to love one another, for he who loves his fellowman has fulfilled the law. The commandments, "Do not commit adultery," "Do not murder," "Do not steal," "Do not covet," and whatever other commandment there may be, are summed up in this one rule: "Love your neighbor as yourself." Love does no harm to its neighbor. Therefore love is the fulfillment of the law.*
>
> —Romans 13:8-10

Forgiveness functions through love. The commandment of love is a requirement, an order, not an option. Love is not an emotion as some may believe it to be, it's a decision that one consciously makes in order to be free of the destruction unforgiveness can bring. If it were based on human emotions, then farewell to relationships of all kinds because emotions change from one day to the next depending upon what mood we find ourselves in. Because they are so unreliable, it's fair to conclude that they can never sustain anything. No, we make a decision to love unconditionally as God has chosen to love us. He has demonstrated for us how to act as a child made in his likeness. He has demonstrated the power to release his forgiveness to us by his grace, and he has given us that same power to release it to others. God's forgiveness is an expression of his love for us.

> *When you were dead in your sins and in the uncircumcision of your sinful nature, God made you alive with Christ. He forgave us all our sins, having canceled the written code, with its regulations, that was against us and that stood opposed to us; he took it away, nailing it to the cross.*
>
> —Colossians 2:13-14

Forgiveness is a spiritual virtue that causes us to rise up against and conquer the evil forces of this fallen world. Nothing can frustrate Satan more than a single act of forgiveness, not only because there's freedom in it, but it works by love, the highest virtue, of which he has set out to destroy. He is fully aware of the power God has given us to release a person through forgiveness. He knows that it restores our soul back to the goodness of our Lord, and through one single act of forgiveness, the highest expression of love is on display and has the power to cause a domino effect. Nothing gives him better honor than the act of unforgiveness. When the goodness of God ceases to flow through you, not only is that a door left unguarded for him and his legions to use to your destruction, but it also hinders the gift of mercy that God had in store for the offender. By this simple act, Satan gets his glory by not only destroying two souls at the price of one, but having an unforgiving heart will also stunt the spiritual growth for both you and the offender and block whatever blessings God had in store for you through forgiveness.

Again, I'm not suggesting that we are to be footstools to the ungodly by just overlooking every act of offense, since those of us who are hidden in Christ, we are one with him, and we wait on God to vindicate the righteous and judge the wicked. But we must stand firm in love, giving respect to God and allowing room for his wrath against evil. To discern that there are spiritual laws operating for us and against us, when someone offends us, we should feel compassion rather than hatred because we know, by spiritual law, that they are summoning to themselves the evil that they portray. We know that a person will reap what they have sown. And if they stand in ignorance of this fact, all the more compassion and mercy we should have for them. As Christ demonstrated,

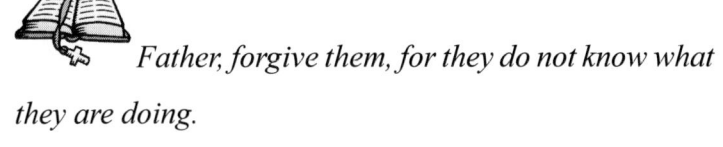

> *Father, forgive them, for they do not know what they are doing.*
>
> —Luke 23:34

By walking in the spirit of love is to live a life of undeniable virtue. It is the highest form of life.

And now these three remain: faith, hope and love. But the greatest of these is love.

—1 Corinthians 13:13

The second is this: "Love your neighbor as yourself." There is no commandment greater than these.

—Mark 12:31

Having spiritual wisdom concerning the spiritual laws that govern every human life, you are able to determine the end of an evil act from the beginning, the destruction one brings upon him or herself by doing evil things. And by this same law, we should be careful of our own actions by choosing our words wisely. They are an expression of our thoughts and a manifestation of our heart.

A fool's lips bring him strife, and his mouth invites a beating.

A fool's mouth is his undoing, and his lips are a snare to his soul.

The words of a gossip are like choice morsels; they go down to a man's inmost parts.

—Proverbs 18:6-8

There is a lesson to be learned in every kind of evil, and our job is to discover it so that we ourselves would not also become enslaved by it.

By this, I mean that we are to never overlook the offender's ability to deceive us by trusting a thief with our house keys or the pedophile with our children or to overlook the abuser's potential to abuse. We ought to gain wisdom from our mistakes and ask God for spiritual discernment.

If any of you lacks wisdom, he should ask God, who gives generously to all without finding fault, and it will be given to him.

—James 1:5

When we feel we have sinned terribly against God, we begin to feel a sense of guilt. That guilt restricts the Holy Spirit from serving its purpose of spiritual restoration by feelings of shame and fear along with other negative emotions. With these emotions, we bring about discord within our bodies, causing it harm. But when we know God has forgiven us, we feel loved; no condemnation, no guilt can destroy our faith. We feel we have been given a second chance, which brings about feelings of joy, repentance, and love. That's your spirit running free like a child in the playground. That's our spirit showing us what it needs to bring us peace and happiness. So if someone is in need of your forgiveness, you have the power to set them free in the same way, bringing forth the blessing of forgiveness for yourself.

> *Do not judge and you will not be judged. Do not condemn, and you will not be condemned. Forgive, and you will be forgiven.*
>
> —Luke 6:37

Truth is, we are all a work in progress, and God deals with us all in according to the condition of our heart in his way in his own time. Take comfort in the spiritual laws and promises that God has provided for our protection and good. Those same laws that apply to you in the same way apply to others. As you're trapped in unforgiveness, the other person has already come before God, confessed his sins, and was set free.

The spirit within is the life flowing through us, serving its purpose by thriving to get us the greater good of happiness through peace and love. So when our emotions are not lined up with the spirit of love, we go against its designed purpose, causing sinful undesirable conditions to develop in our body. That's why you continue to feel uncomfortable about an offense. When you forgive, you feel good, big, powerful, proud, and strong. That's your spirit being set free, bringing you peace. You have then detached yourself from the spirit of darkness and have come into the spirit of life.

If you want forgiveness, give it. If you want happiness, share yours. If you want health, think it, and if you want money, share it, but do it all in the spirit of love and allow the spiritual laws of love to carry you to the greater good of happiness.

Speak and act as those who are going to be judged by the law that brings freedom, because judgment without mercy will be shown to anyone who has not been merciful. Mercy triumphs over judgment.

-James 2:12-13

Do not be surprised, my brothers, if the world hates you. We know that we have passed from death to life, because we love our brothers. Anyone who does not love remains in death. Anyone who hates his brother is a murderer, and you know that no murderer has eternal life in him.

This is how we know what love is: Jesus Christ laid down his life for us. And we ought to lay down our lives for our brothers. If anyone has material possessions and sees his brother in need but has no pity on him, how can the love of God be in him?

Dear children, let us not love with words or tongue but with actions and in truth. This then is how we know that we belong to the truth, and how we set our hearts at rest in his presence, whenever our hearts condemn us. For God is greater than our hearts, and he knows everything.

Dear friends, if our hearts do not condemn us, we have confidence before God and receive from him anything we ask, because we obey his commands and do what pleases him. And this is his command: to believe in the name of his Son, Jesus Christ, and to love one another as he commanded us. Those who obey his commands live in him, and he in them. And this is how we know that he lives in us: We know it by the Spirit he gave us.

—1 John 3:11-24

Chapter 16

The Power Within

All that is beautiful with life was made for us. God has given us the divine power of right thought to bind on earth what has already been established in heaven. He has given us so much through the power of our imagination and faith to create, and yet we accept circumstances and let them navigate our lives as if those circumstances existed before we got here.

We ourselves have the spiritual ability to create very unpleasant conditions in life by living in fear of them and by responding in fear to our circumstances. But if we could learn to put our reasoning aside, we would then begin to understand that the faith used to create our circumstance is the same faith that will change or eliminate them. The solution will always be found within the problem itself.

Every minute of every day we are creating our life in advance through the power of our thoughts by having faith in them, and so the environment and circumstances which we are currently living in is only a direct reflection of the environment and circumstances we hold within our mind. Again, I am not implying that if our thoughts are of perfect peace, we would then, in return, have perfect peace. Nothing in this falling world is perfect. The point to take is although affliction and persecution may come, it is how we respond to it that will be the determining factor of whether it is here to stay or not. When we respond to undesirable circumstances in faith, we locate the lesson it has for us and by doing so, we believe that we are here to serve the higher and greater good in life and so we reject the death that's presented to us by saying, "No! God did not deliver me from the last trial to hand me over to this! If that was the case, he would've left me in the trap in which I last stood."

Our Lord does not contradict himself, nor does he repent of his actions. He is a graceful God who has freely gives us all things. Paul rejected death on many occasions.

> *As it is written, "For your sake we face death all day long; we are considered as sheep to be slaughtered." No! In all these things we are more than conquerors through him who loved us.*
>
> —Romans 8:36-37

When we are oblivious to God's love for us and what he has given us through Christ our Savior, which is the power of faith, our thinking then becomes governed by fear and uncertainty, creating by the law of growth, conditions of worry, insufficiency, and limitations. We tend to blame these conditions on the problem itself when in fact, the condition is not the cause of our life's order, it is the response of fear or faith and the attention we give to the circumstances or events that takes place in our lives, and by doing so we are creating future events of its very nature.

We can never rise above our life's circumstances because it's governed by what we expect. A person cannot succeed with a failure mentality because failure is a condition of the mind, and and since the human mind is ever so eager to express itself, by the law of growth, failure is then created and incorporated if you will, into the life of the person who believes he or she has been defeated. It's a corresponding effect.

Usually when something bad happens we respond in fear, and since every thought is creating our life in advance, conditions of fear becomes a promise for tomorrow, and Satan is always there to confirm it. Our understanding of who we are in Christ is critical to our existence and level of comfort in this life.

Through Christ we have become heirs with him, given in full measure all that he was given in his divine nature.

> *See to it that no one takes you captive through hollow and deceptive philosophy, which depends on human tradition and the basic principles of this world rather than on Christ. For in Christ all the fullness of the Deity lives in bodily form, and you have been given fullness in Christ, who is the head over every power and authority.*
>
> —Colossians 2:8-10

God's love is whole and complete just as our love is for our children. He is not a god of lack, limitations, or disease. He can never create those conditions for his own because he is love, and we, being made in his likeness and image, were created with love. But since one-third of who we are is made of flesh, our thoughts and words become our own, expressing itself through our blood and organs and into our lives' circumstances.

The Bible instructs us to live by faith in every sense of the word. But we tend to apply faith to some things and fear others, and it's because of this fact that we succeed in one area but then fail in the next. There is no grey area between faith and fear. When Jesus said, "Let your yes be yes and your no be no," he intended for us to be stable minded.

But when he asks, he must believe and not doubt, because he who doubts is like a wave of the sea, blown and tossed by the wind. That man should not think he will receive anything from the Lord; he is a double-minded man, unstable in all he does.

—James 1:6-8

Yet there are many Christians who are double minded. They will pray for financial restoration and, at the same, squander the little they have. Faith and deeds is the qualifying factor for your return. Whatever we are praying for in faith must be accompanied by our actions. If it is financial provision, we must use what we have wisely. If it is good health we desire, we must comply with the spiritual and natural laws of health.

Whoever can be trusted with very little can also be trusted with much, and whoever is dishonest with very little will also be dishonest with much. So if you have not been trustworthy in handling worldly wealth, who will trust you with true riches? And if you have not been trustworthy with someone else's property, who will give you property of your own?

—Luke 16:10-12

> *And without faith it is impossible to please God, because anyone who comes to him must believe that he exists and that he rewards those who earnestly seek him.*
>
> —Hebrews 6:11

If we are to ever achieve our highest and greatest good, prayer and faith is the catalyst that will bring it to you. The love God has for you has to be imbedded into your soul without a hint of uncertainty. Yet there are many who are aware of Gods promises but at the time they are unsure of the reality of them so they pray in pity regarding their circumstances. "Lord, I cast all my cares over to you and you know what I want and need, and I don't want much, but all I want is to be able to take care of my children and give them a stable home. If it be your will, please provide, if not, help me to persevere."

This is not a prayer of faith, its a prayer filled with fear and trembling. Satan is god over fear, and he will most certainly show up to honor this fear-based prayer by manipulating circumstances so that your doubt turns into total unbelief.

With this mind-set, you are either unaware of the atonement of Christ and the promises and provisions concerning your life through him or you refuse to believe it to be true for you.

In either case, you limit yourself by your lack understanding of the power of faith. You accept the ministry of Jesus to be true, but you have no real concept of how God orchestrated it for your benefit and so you reject the power within yourself all together; by doing so, you reject the gift of grace.

We can believe by faith that God can heal us if he wants to, but on the other hand, we find it hard to believe that having faith in God's promises will heal us and give us all that we need and more. Because of this mind-set, none of these things can become a reality in our life.

Faith will reveal your answer, the Bible says, and since this is true, the answer will always be *yes* as long as the request is in line with what he already provided by his grace.

In John 16:23, Jesus said, "My father will give you whatever you ask in my name. Until now you have not asked for anything in my name. Ask and you will receive and your joy will be complete."

In Mark 11:24, Jesus said, "Whatever you ask in my name, believe that you have received it and it will be yours."

By the grace of the almighty God, Jesus came to restore the blessing that was lost through Adam and put it back into our hands through faith. The blessing is available to us all, but in order to walk in the blessing, we have to receive it by faith, just as we received our invisible God himself.

> *Humble yourselves, therefore, under the mighty hand of God so that at the proper time he may exalt you, casting all your anxieties on him, because he cares for you. Be sober-minded, be watchful. Your adversary the devil prowls around like a roaring lion, seeking someone to devour. Resist him, firm in your faith, knowing that the same kinds of suffering are being experienced by your brotherhood throughout the world. And after you have suffered a little while, the God of all grace, who has called you to his eternal glory in Christ, will himself restore, confirm, strengthen, and establish you. To him be the dominion forever and ever. Amen.*
>
> —1 Peter 5:6-11

Chapter 17

Breaking the Cycle

Far too long have we let the conditions of our natural life reshape who God has created us to be. Everything we choose to accomplish in this life requires some kind of training; whether it's for a job or a career, we must learn all there is to learn about that thing in order to be skillful and successful.

Well, the same rule applies to your life. The training manual to life is the Bible (Book of Instructions Before Leaving Earth). This book is not the instruction manual for life in heaven, on the contrary, it instructs us on how we should live here on earth.

We grow up driven by the physical things we see around us, never truly coming to a complete understanding of their God given purpose. So we spend a lifetime speaking idle words, thinking deadly thoughts, operating spiritual principles we don't acknowledge or understand to own destruction.

We embrace the lower standards of life, accepting illness, addiction and obesity calling it hereditary. We work hard most of our life, not having the faith to live out the passion God has placed in our hearts, and so we end up with a lifetime full of regrets, never fully living up to our true potential. This is because the Spirit within us desires to live a life worthy of its intended purpose which is to not only bring us into partnership with our creator by bringing the things we desire to life, but in assisting us to serve a higher purpose for the common good of the whole. But because we have chosen to eliminate its function in our lives whether it was done consciously or subconsciously, the human spirit remained bound by the conditions of our mind, without expression. It becomes likened to a caged lion held against its will. And it is because of this desire for expression one will continue to have regrets. Its your spirits way of telling you that you were meant to be more than you are. But a person that has no spiritual discernment is not equipped to recognize that gnawing at the flesh (regret) as a sign of higher living. So they reduce it to fantasy.

Because of this faithless mind set, they conclude that if God wanted them to have more, he would've given them more.

The truth is he did; we were never rightfully taught how to claim it by faith. If it's true that we were all created by God, made in his image and likeness, wouldn't it be sensible to find out who we are by examining the nature of God himself and learn how to live in this physical body through him?

He put us here, we are his creation, and he has the basic instructions for life and how it is to be lived in its highest form. We have answers for everything we created except life and how it operates. This is because man didn't create life and had no idea of how it works unless we look to God himself for guidance.

Sure, its more convenient and less convicting to sit back and blame God and all sorts of things and people for our failures, shortcomings, and destruction. But what we have failed at seeing is the the destruction we have brought to ourselves by rejecting his truth and lesson that's within the very thing that has the appearance of death. We can spend a lifetime trying to master the human body but will never get it right without coming to a complete understanding of the human spirit and its divine purpose.

The Bible teaches us *"right thought, long life."* Your body needs your mind to participate in its purpose of life in order for the body to function properly.

Conditions of lack, poverty, limitations, and disease cannot be God's plan for your life. If it were then it would be wrong to seek health care and financial provision. It would also be wrong to dream. All these things would be considered sin in the eyes of God had he placed these conditions on you.

God said to Joshua, "Meditate on my words day and night and observe to do all that is written and you will make your way prosperous and successful." The power was with him all along; it was in his mind and in his mouth.

If you can see another person living abundantly, with everything he or she could ever dream of, creating things beyond your own comprehension, living a healthy lifestyle, they were not created as special human beings. God said, "Let all nations of this earth be blessed through the faith of Abraham." This power came through faith in their creative ability.

While we are wasting precious life accepting the lowest level of life instead of the abundant life that God has truly dealt to us, living in doubt and unbelief and insufficiency, God has been trying to show us who we are through the power and the creative minds of others. We were put here as equals therefore no one can never be favored over the other. It is true that from the beginning God has chosen certain individuals to do dis will and to prophesy his word. But their hearts were receptive to it. Remember the story of King Saul? He was chosen by God and anointed by a messenger of God by the name of Nathan. Although he was willing to carry out the will of God, he rebelled against God by proceeding with his own plans. For this reason, God took away his anointing and kingdom and handed it over to a 17yr old boy name David instead who had such a heart for God that he defeated a giant with a stone and a sling shot believing that the power of God was with him.

This example tell us that if your not willing to do his will, he will find someone that is.

We should all spend our best energy in understanding the gift of creation that God has equally distributed amongst us all and seeking out his plan for us. Why concern yourself with the issue of race or if Jesus was white or black in the natural? Does it matter in the spiritual realm? If we were all made in God's likeness and image, is it really possible for our blood to be tainted or destroyed by other races? Are we not all born of the same substance and purpose? No matter if we're black or white, we will always give birth to a natural human being.

You are all sons of God through faith in Christ Jesus, for all of you who were baptized into Christ have clothed yourselves with Christ. There is neither Jew nor

> *Greek, slave nor free, male nor female, for you are all one in Christ Jesus.*
>
> —Galatians 3:26-28

Whoever you are, wherever you are, you will never have access to the things of God without learning how to live through his spirit that lives within you. We cannot proclaim to be children of God and at the same time, live in the yoke of the enemy because Jesus has defeated the enemy for those who were held captive to him so that he would no longer have power over us. So why proclaim to be a child of God and yet live as though you are not? How could a child of God live any longer in bondage knowing that we have victory over Satan through Christ our savior? It's a clear contradiction of what Christ has done and a vicious scheme that belongs to Satan.

> *As for you, you were dead in your transgressions and sins, in which you used to live when you followed the ways of this world and of the ruler of the kingdom of the air (Satan) the spirit who is now at work in those who are disobedient. All of us also lived among them at one time, gratifying the cravings of our sinful nature and following its desires and thoughts. Like the rest, we were by nature objects of wrath. But because of his great love for us, God, who is rich in mercy, made us alive with*

Christ even when we were dead in transgressions—it is by grace you have been saved. And God raised us up with Christ and seated us with him in the heavenly realms in Christ Jesus, in order that in the coming ages he might show the incomparable riches of his grace, expressed in his kindness to us in Christ.

—Ephesians 2:1-7

There should be a clear distinction between those who are in Christ and those who are of the world. The thing that has trapped the people of this world and led them into bondage is their inheritance for disobedience. But those of us who are in Christ should no longer share in the sufferings of this world. Though they may come, they should never harm us because God delivers those who are faithful to him.

I became a servant of this gospel by the gift of God's grace given me through the working of his power. Although I am less than the least of all God's people, this grace was given me: to preach to the Gentiles the unsearchable riches of Christ, and to make plain to everyone the administration of this mystery, which for ages past was kept hidden in God, who created all things.

—Ephesians 3:7

What price tag are you willing to put on your soul? There is only one person who knows how to give you the greater good of happiness, and that's God working through the Holy Spirit within you. That *intuitive nudge* spiritual teachers speak of is not the *universe responding* to your thoughts, it's the Holy Spirit operating through spiritual principles and without God, whatever you build will fall.

Let's break the cycle of false beliefs and circumstance. Let's start learning how to live in abundance according to our desires set by God, not the limitations set by man. Let's start retraining our thoughts and the thoughts of our children to God's word and will. Search the book of life for God's will in regards to your life and stand firm in God's promise to bring it to pass.

If you are unsure of this power or believe that your current state is a reality and unchangeable, take hold of whatever physical object you believe to be a reality and break it, then ask yourself, "Is this still a reality?" Your answer should be no, and this act should symbolize the power you have to change your circumstances.

Search the Bible for your former way of thinking and living and you will surely see that if your mind set is in harmony with the ways of this world, your way of thinking attracts every kind of evil and goes against God's word and promises which is the very reason destruction has hit your life.

Stop believing that you can say anything without it having an effect on your physical body and life. Start with Proverbs from the beginning to end, and you will see your own true life unfold before your very eyes and realize that your heart is the cause and your life order is the effect.

> *For from within, out of men's hearts, come evil thoughts, sexual immorality, theft, murder, adultery, greed, malice, deceit, lewdness, envy, slander, arrogance and folly. All these evils come from inside and make a man "unclean."*
>
> —Mark 7:21-23

> *The good man brings good things out of the good stored up in him, and the evil man brings evil things out of the evil stored up in him. But I tell you that men will have to give account on the day of judgment for every careless word they have spoken. For by your words you will be acquitted, and by your words you will be condemned.*
>
> —Matthew 12:35-37

Above all else, guard your heart, for it is the wellspring of life.

-Proverbs 4:23

If you cannot see how everything is brought into existence from the unseen through the power of our thoughts and words, then look around you; everything you thought was possible in your life, don't you have it? From the clothes on your back to the reality of your circumstances. You saw it as a reality for you and so it came to you. That's what faith is. This goes for sickness and disease as well. In many cases, you have spoken the very thing you dread into existence by giving it attention and establishing it through words. In other cases, they have accepted what Satan has presented to the as truth and so the condition will remain until they learn otherwise.

Now that you are aware, change the things you don't want in your life. Dream bigger dreams and hold them, meditate on them, and claim them through spiritual words with spiritual truth. Do not allow your current conditions to take its stand in your life. Rise up above them through the power of right thought. If you're laboring to be rich, you're laboring in the wrong direction. Labor for God through the purification of your heart and you would see that all that you need would follow.

Let's put a stop to generational cures by teaching our children not to say words like "I can't, that's impossible." Let's begin to train them with words of encouragement. Get out of their mind's hereditary ailments; let them know that they are not like you or anyone, but they are like God. What benefit would it be for us to be an example for our children if our life is a struggle? No! They are made in the image and likeness of the almighty God. Teach them that what they *believe* is what they get and not the other way around.

As for me and my house, I instruct my children to repeat after me whether they want to or not. It's the seed that counts; the spirit of God is responsible for its growth and vitality and operates according to his will. They are not allowed to say words or phrases like "I'm sick or I'm dead serious, it's killing me, I hate that, I can't or it doesn't look like it to me." When they ask me about our families' hereditary illnesses, I explain to them who they are in Christ and the victory they have over everything in life, that God has given each newborn child a chance for perfect health regardless of what their family experienced.

I believe God; therefore, I choose life for me and my family.

Chapter 18

Unity

Everyone has a story and a gift of their own that should be shared with the world. I believe that every human being has been given this gift by God. The problem is that most of us feel we have nothing to give. We live our lives believing that in order to give to another person, we have to be complete within ourselves, not lacking anything. In this state of mind, we exist only to please ourselves and our loved ones, and never serve our true God intended purpose, which is to first obey God, by loving one another and to be of service.

We have become so self-destructive that we are unable to recognize God's divine order. He has placed people, circumstances, and events in our lives for our spiritual and physical nourishment, and we have rebuked most of them, deeming these situations and people hazardous to our health and well-being, ignorant to the fact that we were to grow and learn from every experience given. Most people would rather have complete control over who they are to accept into their lives in order to control the conditions in which they live. These people lack spiritual discernment. God knows what you need. And in his great wisdom, he sends people into your life for the benefit of your spiritual growth.

Reaching for the highest and best life has to offer *is* God's will for us, but our journey to this never-ending high place is not our own, for what real value would our pitfalls, trials, and tribulations have if we kept them to ourselves. Once we've learned from our mistakes, it's likely we won't tread upon that road again, but and if we find ourselves repeating our mistakes, our subconscious mind will always hold the experience. The truth is, our journeys will always be of greater value and benefit to someone else to serve a far greater purpose.

But during this process we tend to be oblivious in our ability to give or to be of service to anyone but ourselves mostly by default. Most of us were never taught to consider the well being of others as a reflection of ourselves. Some people believe that when and if they strike it rich, only then will they be able to meet the needs of others, mainly their family and a few close friends. Others declare, "How can I give when I can hardly meet the needs of my own?" Then there are the rich young rulers who have it made also by default, who spend most of their time in "*me*" mode, and who have accountants that occasionally give to various charitable organizations in hopes to gain more recognition from the public.

The Bible teaches us that we all have something to give, no matter what the circumstances are in our lives. To be quite honest, most will never reach their full potential, and the ones that do find their purpose usually find it later in life as I did.

Looking back on my life, I have to admit to being a selfish, egotistical, self-absorbed person who had a negative effect on nearly everyone I came in contact with. I chose to charge my past to trial and error in preparation for now, in doing so, I am able to embrace my former destructive ways in a way that allows me to accept and appreciate whom I've become in Christ today. In all honesty, if I had to do my life all over again, there are definitely some things that I would surely avoid, but I can't see me being happy where I am today without my past being the way it was.

The Bible teaches us that we are all the body of Christ, that he is the head, but we are the body made complete by many parts, and because of this truth, one body part cannot antagonize or cut off the other without affecting the whole. In other words, you would not cut off your own hand knowing it is of great value and benefit to you. Well, the same thing is true with people. We were all put here to be of service to one another with different kinds of gifts to offer, and when they are accepted by those who were destined to receive them, life then becomes your oyster. You will begin to appreciate people by acknowledging their value and purpose for your benefit.

Closed-minded people are self-absorbed people who hate socializing. If you would notice, their behavior and isolation from the public is a clear indication that they believe they need no one, and their social circle is limited to people they have been around for decades. If you are content in this setting, not wanting anymore than what you already have, this would be an ideal environment for you. But for those of us who want to reach our greatest and higher good, we need to expand our social circle in order to exchange the God giving gifts and talents needed for success in every area of life. We were not put here as a whole to function independent of each other.

Let me give an example. Our spirit needs our soul for expression. Our thoughts take form in our mind. The mind uses the brain to store our thoughts. The brain uses the spine to express those thoughts and to deliver vital information to the body for its function and well-being. All the functions of the body from the atoms to the organs all work together as a unit, and when one part is damaged and dies, the rest of the body suffers the consequences and the life of that body becomes limited in comparison to a healthy, complete body. But the body is totally dependent upon the brain for its survival which is the head. It is the high priest and lord over the body and demands that the body work as a unit in order to function in the perfection in which it was created to function.

The same scenario is true as a people. We were not created to function, grow, and develop alone. We *are* the *body of Christ,* the workers, and he is the head, and although we were created independent of one another, we are created for each other in order to achieve our own greatest and highest good. We can never get there without the help of one another. Just like the body, if one part fails to provide the necessary service needed for my growth, I would be hindered in my success.

We are one under God. Jesus needed us in order to bring glory to the father. Our heavenly father gave him a mission to accomplish. He was sent here to descend as a man in order to take back the dominion and authority that God had given Adam who in turn lost it to Satan. After overcoming the world, he put back into our hands what was lost and ascended back on high to sit at the right hand of God and was crowned the high priest and Lord over us all. He was given the world and everything in it. Due to his obedience, he was put even higher than the angels. Because he suffered in his body for us, God declared that no one will come to the father except through his son, the Christ. Jesus declared that whosoever should follow him would receive eternal life with him, the Holy Spirit as a guide here on earth, and would enter into the kingdom of heaven which lies within us. In this kingdom, there is peace, wisdom, righteousness, sanctification, and redemption.

All this was accomplished out of an act of obedience to the head. He could not see himself separate from his father. But in order to accomplish his highest and greatest good, he had to descend as a natural man, to share in our pain, suffering, and wash us of sin in order to restore life's order. But notice how he needed us to do it.

The two greatest commandments is first to love the Lord with all your heart. The second is to love your neighbor as you would love yourself. So in order to love God, we have to accept his ways, obey him, and follow his orders. In order to love our neighbors, we have to treat them as we would want to be treated. And what do we all want? *Service!* Help in time of need. Love, sympathy, respect, and equality. Other gifts of service include teachers, pastors, mentors, counselors, bankers, farmers, doctors, scientist, inventors, and so on. So I ask you, does any one person provide all these services?

Only Jesus could provide all the services a man could ever need. And these services are still available but only in *the body of Christ.*

Me plus you and you and you equals a *whole*. Now that I have acknowledged that I need you in order to coexist and live to my fullest potential as Jesus did, would it make much sense to deny your role in my life? Would I now say, "*Forget about you, I don't need you*"? How about I put some corresponding action to that statement by cutting off my own right arm? It's the same thing. It's what the law *seedtime and harvest* is founded on.

We are all members of the same body serving one head, each equipped with a gift of service of some kind or another. Our gifts are not our own; they are to be brought into full expression that it might add to the life of others.

What most people fail to realize is that God brings about gifts, blessings, and answered prayers in a multitude of forms by using people, places, and circumstances.

As an example, one will pray for patience, but after praying, they forget the request made. So they go on with life aggravated, murmuring, "I always end up in situations like this, I hate it. I've been asking God for patience for years, and I still have none! I guess he will change me when he's ready!" What you fail to realize is that he has already answered your prayers by bringing about the very circumstances you are frustrated about in order to help you develop your patience. You have disconnected yourself from the people and circumstances God created to help you by looking at them as hindrance as opposed to blessings or answered prayers.

You see, many of us have unrealistic, unconscious notions about God and his deliverance. Because he's so majestic and powerful, when we pray realistic prayers for our salvation, we close our eyes and miss the opportunity given for our salvation due to our unconscious high expectation of a miraculous, supernatural, instantaneous delivery. We are natural, physical people who are made to develop into what ever we are to become, otherwise, we relapse back into what we are trying to be delivered from.

Here's a common story that will testify to this fact.

God has the power to deliver us miraculously, instantaneously from anything, and he is not in need people to do it for him; however, he chooses the option to deliver us first by way of people, in hopes that we may know how valuable we all are to each other and by this we develop over time into accepting his commandment of love.

When we pray for patience, God will not pour it out of the sky into our laps, he provides us the *opportunity* to *develop* our patience. You miss the call every time. When we pray for unity in our homes, he will not swing a rope from heaven and bind you together with that loved one you long to be close with. He will bring about the opportunity for you to get close with that person. If we pray for financial provision, he will not put a check in your mail box by visualization and meditation as the secret team suggest. He will instead provide you the opportunity to become financially established, but only in accordance with your ability to rightly manage what he has already given you.

> "Whoever can be trusted with very little can also be trusted with much, and whoever is dishonest with very little will also be dishonest with much. So if you have not been trustworthy in handling worldly wealth, who will trust you with true riches? And if you have not been trustworthy with someone else's property, who will give you property of your own?
>
> —Like 16:10-12

I believe God has an intended individual purpose for us all, but when one is spiritually discerned, they are unable to connect to their purpose, so they let life take them wherever the wind blows. Those who recognize their purpose pursue it and serve it, but for those who don't are used in my eyes as *extras* if you will. Like movie castings, you're called to serve a different purpose day to day. In this subconscious mind-set, you get blessings for side jobs that you had no idea were ordained for you, and your disclaimer is "I don't know what's going on, but after I helped that lady with her bags, I found a $20 bill on my way home, hmm, who knew?"

It's like the body and its vital functions. Atoms, cells, organs, and tissues are vital to life but our exterior physical body parts are extras. We don't necessary need any of our limbs to survive; however, they are beneficial to our livelihood.

The body is a unit, though it is made up of many parts; and though all its parts are many, they form one body. So it is with Christ. For we were all baptized by one Spirit into one body—whether Jews or Greeks, slave or free—and we were all given the one Spirit to drink.

Now the body is not made up of one part but of many. If the foot should say, "Because I am not a hand, I do not belong to the body," it would not for that reason cease to be part of the body. And if the ear should say, "Because I am not an eye, I do not belong to the body," it would not for that reason cease to be part of the body. If the whole body were an eye, where would the sense of hearing be? If the whole body were an ear, where would the sense of smell be? But in fact God has arranged the parts in the body, every one of them, just as he wanted them to be. If they were all one part, where would the body be? As it is, there are many parts, but one body.

The eye cannot say to the head, "I don't need you!" And the head cannot say to the heart, "I don't need you!" On the contrary, those parts of the body that seem to be weaker are indispensable, and the parts that we think are less honorable we treat with special honor. And the parts that are unpresentable are treated with special modesty, while our presentable parts need no special treatment.

But God has combined the members of the body and has given greater honor to the parts that lacked it, so that there should be no division in the body, but that its parts should have equal concern for each other. If one part suffers, every part suffers with it; if one part is honored, every part rejoices with it.

Now you are the body of Christ, and each one of you is a part of it. And in the church God has appointed first of all apostles, second prophets, third teachers, then workers of miracles, also those having gifts of healing, those able to help others, those with gifts of administration, and those speaking in different kinds of tongues. Are all apostles? Are all prophets? Are all teachers? Do all work miracles?

Do all have gifts of healing? Do all speak in tongues? Do all interpret? But eagerly desire the greater gifts. And now I will show you the most excellent way.

—1 Corinthians 12: 12-30

If I speak in the tongues of men and of angels, but have not love, I am only a resounding gong or a clanging cymbal. If I have the gift of prophecy and can fathom all mysteries and all knowledge, and if I have a faith that can move mountains, but have not love, I am nothing. If I give all I possess to the poor and surrender my body to the flames, but have not love, I gain nothing. Love is patient, love is kind. It does not envy, it does not boast, it is not proud.

5It is not rude, it is not self–seeking, it is not easily angered, it keeps no record of wrongs.

6Love does not delight in evil but rejoices with the truth. It always protects, always trusts, always hopes, always perseveres. Love never fails. But where there are prophecies, they will cease; where there are tongues, they will be stilled; where there is knowledge, it will pass away. For we know in part and we prophesy in part, but when perfection comes, the imperfect disappears. 11When I was a child, I talked like a child, I thought like a child, I reasoned like a child. When I became a man, I put childish ways behind me. Now we see but a poor reflection as in a mirror; then we shall see face to face. Now I know in part; then I shall know fully, even as I am fully known. And now these three remain: faith, hope and love. But the greatest of these is love.

1 Corinthians 13: 1-13

Author's Note

Let me just say that I know how these things must sound to the average person. Because my teachings are contrary to what you have always believed, I expect that my teachings will be difficult to accept. I too became mystified as I familiarized myself with the teachings of our Creator. They opposed everything I have ever known to be true. As I hungrily search God's word for answers pertaining to specific issues about my own life in general, God has revealed to me through his word his infallible truths in just about every area of life. But I had a choice to believe it or leave it. That decision cost me my most valuable possessions such as my opinion, my pride, self-preservation, and will. It changed the entire course of my life for the better. I began to compare his word to my life, and as I looked back at how I used to live and where I ended up, it became crystal clear that these spiritual principles that God spoke of in his word was operating in my life all along. Every bad circumstance I have ever experienced was foretold through scripture, and with every effect, the cause was revealed whether the cause was within myself or me just being victimized by the over powering will of another human being. It was no denying the truth. My actions along with the actions of others in regards to my childhood, mirrored the cause and the circumstance mirrored the effect.

I will never claim to have all the answers for everything that happens throughout a person's lifetime, nor do I make any claim of being medically trained in mental or physical health. But there is one thing that I am certain of, and that's God's infallible truth. He is the author of the human life. His truths stand above man's logic. Through it, I found the cause behind many of life's circumstances good and bad. After thousands of hours of intense study, God has qualified me as an author of truth, and with it, I was faced with another choice. Terrified that the world would deem me unqualified, I stepped out in faith and did what God has ask me to do which is to write this book in spite of my lack of education and trust that he will do the rest. I take no credit for this work therefore I need no special recognition. I humble myself under his authority and consider myself a lowly seed sower. My only hope is that through this book, God will reach those who are destined to receive this message of hope as I try to wrap my head around his decision to use me.

How magnificent is his work that he would completely change the order of which my life was heading in exchange for the order that he predestined it to be? My former aspirations have been wiped from my memory. Praise be to God the Creator and father of us all.

I urge my reader to closely examine *their own life* against what is being taught through this book.

Edwards Brothers, Inc.
Thorofare, NJ USA
May 18, 2011